SHRM-CP/SCP
EXAM PREP MASTERY
2024-25 Edition

SHRM STUDY GUIDE WITH 450+ PRACTICE QUESTIONS, 100+ PIC-WISE TABLES WITH EXAMPLES, PROVEN STRATEGIES, AND TIPS FOR FIRST-TIME SUCCESS

R. FANATOMY

BONUS BOOKLET INCLUDED

copyright@ dr. fanatomy 2024

All rights reserved. No part of this publication may be reproduced, distributed, or transmitted in any form or by any means, including photocopying, recording, or other electronic or mechanical methods, without the prior written permission of the publisher, except in the case of brief quotations embodied in critical reviews and certain other noncommercial uses permitted by copyright law.

This book is a work of non-fiction, and any resemblance to actual persons, living or dead, or actual events is purely coincidental.

The information and techniques described in this book are intended for educational and informational purposes only. The author and publisher shall not be held liable for any injury, damage, or loss arising from using or misusing the information presented in this book.

While every effort has been made to ensure the accuracy of the information contained within this book, the author and publisher make no warranties or representations express or implied, about the completeness, accuracy, reliability, suitability, or availability with respect to the contents of this book for any purpose. The use of any information provided in this book is at the reader's own risk.

Declaration

I am delighted to introduce you to "SHRM-CP/SCP Exam Prep Mastery.

This book has been meticulously crafted to provide the essential knowledge and strategies to excel in the SHRM Certified Professional (CP) or Senior Certified Professional (SCP) exam.

It is important to clarify that this book is an unofficial resource. While our team has dedicated extensive efforts to ensure its alignment with SHRM's exam objectives, it is not an official publication endorsed or sanctioned by the Society for Human Resource Management (SHRM).

Therefore, as you embark on your journey to prepare for the SHRM CP/SCP exam, you must exercise discernment in utilizing this guide. While our content aims to complement your study efforts, we strongly recommend supplementing it with official SHRM materials, such as the SHRM Learning System and resources available on the SHRM website, to ensure a comprehensive understanding of exam content.

Furthermore, we emphasize the ethical and responsible use of this resource. Success in the SHRM CP/SCP exam requires a solid foundation in HR principles and practices. This book supports your preparation efforts and should not be considered a substitute for thorough study or professional development.

As authors and publishers of this guide, we must emphasize that we are not liable for any inaccuracies, omissions, or misinterpretations in the content presented. Additionally, any decisions or actions taken based on the information provided are the reader's sole responsibility.

Recognizing the dynamic nature of SHRM's policies and regulations is also essential. While we strive to keep this guide updated, changes in SHRM exam content or guidelines may occur. We urge you to stay informed of developments by regularly consulting official SHRM resources.

By utilizing this guide, you acknowledge and accept the aforementioned statements. We trust you will approach your SHRM CP/SCP exam preparation with dedication, integrity, and a commitment to excellence.

Wishing you success in your SHRM CP/SCP exam journey.

Don't forget to download the Bonus Booklet

Table of Content

- Choosing the right SHRM Exam: SCP or CP (1)

- Glossary (2-6)

- Situational Judgment Items (SJIs) for the SHRM CP/SCP Exam (7)

- SHRM Certification Exams: Most Important Aspect of Preparation (8)

- Top 5 SHRM Certification Exam Prep Tips (9)

- Conquering the SHRM Certification Exam (10)

- Maintaining Your SHRM Certification (11-12)

- **271**- Question-Answer Notes for SHRM Exam (13-53)

Download via link or QR code

https://bit.ly/SHRMBONUS

TABLE OF CONTENTS

1. ALL ABOUT THE EXAM- INTRODUCTION (4-10)

- Basic Questions of Exam Takers
- What is SHRM-BASK
- 9 Behavioral Competencies
- Technical Competency
- About SHRM Certified Professional (SCM-CP)Certification
- About SHRM Senior Certified Professional (SHRM-SCP)Certification

2. EXAM PATTERN: SHRM-CP &SCP (11-18)

- SHRM -CP Exam Format
- SHRM-CP Exam Registration
- Tips to Pass the SHRM Exam
- SHRM CP/SCP Exam Scoring
- SHRM-CP Exam Composition
- SHRM-CP Exam Question Types
- SHRM -SCP Exam Format
- SHRM-SCP Exam Composition
- SHRM-SCP Exam Question Types

3. BEHAVIORAL COMPETENCIES- LEADERSHIP CLUSTER(19-56)

Leadership Cluster

- **Leadership & Navigation**
  - Navigating the Organization
  - Vision
  - Managing HR Initiatives
  - Influence
  - *Quiz Corner 1 and Solution*

- **Ethical Practice**
  - Personal Integrity
  - Professional Integrity
  - Ethical Agent
  - *Quiz Corner 2 and Solution*

- **Diversity, Equity & Inclusion**
  - Creating a Diverse and Inclusive Culture
  - Ensuring Equity Effectiveness
  - Connecting DE&I to
  - Organizational Performance
  - *Quiz Corner 3 and Solution*

4. BEHAVIORAL COMPETENCIES- INTERPERSONAL CLUSTER (57-102)

Interpersonal Cluster

- **Relationship Management**
    - *Networking*
    - *Relationship Building*
    - *Teamwork*
    - *Negotiation*
    - *Conflict Management*
    - **Quiz Corner 4 and Solution**

- **Communication**
    - *Delivering Messages*
    - *Exchanging Organizational Information*
    - *Listening*
    - **Quiz Corner 5 and Solution**

- **Global Mindset**
    - *Operating in a Culturally Diverse Workplace*
    - *Operating in a Global Environment*
    - *Advocating for a Culturally Diverse and Inclusive Workplace*
    - **Quiz Corner 6 and Solution**

5. BEHAVIORAL COMPETENCIES- BUSINESS CLUSTER (103-140)

Business Cluster

- **Business Acumen**
    - *Business and Competitive Awareness*
    - *Business Analysis*
    - *Strategic Alignment*
    - **Quiz Corner 7 and Solution**

- **Consultation**
    - *Delivering Business Challenges*
    - *Designing HR Solutions*
    - *Advising on HR Solutions*
    - *Change Management*
    - *Service Excellence*
    - **Quiz Corner 8 and Solution**

5. BEHAVIORAL COMPETENCIES- BUSINESS CLUSTER (103-140)

Business Cluster

- **Analytical Aptitude**
    - Data Advocate
    - Data Gathering
    - Data Analysis
    - Evidence-Based Decision-Making
    - **Quiz Corner 9 and Solution**

6. DOMAIN 1: PEOPLE KNOWLEDGE (141-160)

- HR Strategy
- Talent Acquisition
- Employee Engagement & Retention
- Learning & Development
- Total Rewards
- **Quiz Corner 10 and Solution**

7. DOMAIN 2: ORGANIZATION KNOWLEDGE (161-179)

- Structure of the HR Function
- Organizational Effectiveness & Development
- Workforce Management
- Employee & Labor Relations
- Technology Management
- **Quiz Corner 11 and Solution**

8. DOMAIN 3: WORKPLACE KNOWLEDGE (180-195)

- Managing a Global Workforce
- Risk Management
- Corporate Social Responsibility
- U.S. Employment Law & Regulations
- **Quiz Corner 12 and Solution**

9. APPENDIX & CONCLUSION (196-205)

- *Glossary*
- *Sample Study Plan*
- *Conclusion*

10. SAMPLE QUESTIONS FOR THE EXAM (206-214)

- *Sample Question & Solution SHRM CP*
- *Sample Question & Solution SHRM SCP*

1. ALL ABOUT THE EXAM- BASIC QUERIES OF THE APPLICANTS

1. SHRM-CP & SCP - BASIC INFO

This chapter focuses on inquiring about all the necessary preliminary information from a potential candidate.

Basic Questions of Exam Takers

What is SHRM certification, and why is it significant in HR?

- *SHRM certification is the HR certification offered by the world's largest HR membership organization.*
- *It is competency-based, focusing on the knowledge and behaviors crucial for HR professionals.*
- *SHRM-certified individuals are recognized as experts and leaders in HR and enjoy higher credibility, salaries, and career success.*

What are the differences between SHRM-CP and SHRM-SCP?

- *SHRM-CP is for individuals performing HR-related duties or pursuing a career in HR management.*
- *SHRM-SCP is for those engaged in strategic-level HR-related work.*

How do SHRM-CP and SHRM-SCP exams assess competence in HR?

- *The exams evaluate an individual's competency as an HR practitioner in the evolving world of work.*
- *They are designed to reflect the challenges of HR work.*

What is the recommended method of preparation for SHRM exams?

- *Please start with the SHRM BASK (the blueprint for the exam) and pair it with the SHRM Learning System.*
- *Utilize additional SHRM resources such as prep courses, study guides, and practice item workbooks.*

When do most applicants decide to apply and study for SHRM exams?

- *Applicants typically decide to apply and start studying about 3-4 months before the exam.*

What is the structure of SHRM exams?

- *Exam appointments are scheduled for 4 hours.*
- *Actual testing comprises 3 hours and 40 minutes, with 20 minutes allocated for pre- and post-exam activities.*
- *Ninety percent of candidates complete the exam within the allotted time.*

What is SHRM-BASK

(**SHRM B**ody of **A**pplied **S**kills and **K**nowledge)

Origins of SHRM BASK:

- In 2011, SHRM initiated extensive research involving thousands of HR professionals to identify critical competencies for HR success.

- This led to the development of the initial SHRM Competency Model, defining eight behavioral competencies and one technical competency.

Evolution to SHRM BASK:

- The SHRM Competency Model emphasizes behavioral competencies crucial for HR success. The SHRM Body of Applied Skills and Knowledge (SHRM BASK) further refines this model by delineating knowledge areas alongside behavioral competencies.

- The updated version, released in 2021, comprises **9 behavioral competencies** and **1 technical competency divided into 14 functional areas.**

9 Behavioral Competencies

Leadership Cluster	Interpersonal Cluster	Business Cluster
Leadership and Navigation	Relationship Management	Business Acumen
Ethical Practice	Communication	Consultation
Diversity, Equity, and Inclusion	Global Mindset	Analytical Aptitude

Technical Competency

The HR Expertise competency is one technical competency which outlines **14 functional areas grouped into three domains.**

Domain 1: People Knowledge	Domain 2: Organizational Knowledge	Domain 3: Workplace Knowledge
HR Strategy	Structure of the HR Function	Managing a Global Workforce
Talent Acquisition	Organizational Effectiveness and Development	Risk Management
Employee Engagement and Retention	Workforce Management	Corporate Social Responsibility
Learning and Development	Employee Labor and Relations	US Employment Law and Regulations
Total Rewards	Technology Management	

Role of SHRM BASK in Certification:

The SHRM BASK defines content areas for SHRM's certification exams:

- SHRM Certified Professional (SHRM-CP®) for **operational** HR roles.
- SHRM Senior Certified Professional (SHRM-SCP®) for **strategic** HR roles.

Framework for Exam Development:

- SHRM BASK is the framework for item writers developing SHRM-CP and SHRM-SCP exam questions.
- It guides individuals and organizations in creating exam preparation materials.

About SHRM Certified Professional (SCM-CP) Certification

Intended Audience:

- SHRM Certified Professional (SHRM-CP®) certification suits individuals performing HR/HR-related duties.
- It's also applicable for currently enrolled students and those pursuing a career in Human Resource Management.

Eligibility Criteria:

- Candidates for SHRM-CP certification do not need to hold an HR title.
- No degree or previous HR experience is required, although a basic working knowledge of HR practices and principles is recommended.
- Alternatively, a degree from an Academically Aligned program is also acceptable.

Exam Focus:

- The SHRM-CP exam assesses competency in HR at the operational level.

- This involves implementing policies, supporting day-to-day HR functions, and acting as an HR point of contact for staff and stakeholders.

Proficiency Standards:

- Refer to the SHRM Body of Applied Skills and Knowledge (SHRM BASK®) for detailed information on proficiency standards.

- Proficiency Indicators are provided for all HR professionals, guiding candidates in understanding the credential requirements.

Job Role Characteristics:

- A SHRM-CP is suitable for individuals performing HR or HR-related duties.

- The nature of the work is operational, involving policy implementation and serving as the day-to-day HR point person.

- Duties are typically specialized rather than general.

About SHRM Senior Certified Professional (SCM-SCP) Certification

Audience and Work Profile:

- The SHRM Senior Certified Professional (SHRM-SCP) certification targets individuals with specific work duties. These duties may include developing HR policies or procedures, overseeing integrated HR operations, directing HR enterprises, or aligning HR strategies with organizational goals.

Eligibility Criteria & Experience Requirements:

- Applicants should have at least three years performing strategic-level HR duties.

- Alternatively, SHRM-CP holders with at least three years of experience in or transitioning to strategic roles are eligible.

- Applicants must demonstrate at least 1,000 hours of strategic-level HR work per calendar year.

- Part-time work qualifies as long as the 1,000-hour standard is met.

- Experience may be salaried or hourly, and HR consultants can demonstrate qualifying experience through their client work.

- Holding an HR title or having a degree is not mandatory for SHRM-SCP candidates.

Job Role Characteristics:

- A SHRM-SCP is suitable for individuals leading HR operations or engaging in strategic HR work.

- Strategic-level work involves driving culture, creating HR strategy, developing policy, etc.

Exam Focus:

- The SHRM-SCP exam assesses competency in strategic-level HR work.

- This includes developing HR policies/procedures, overseeing HR operations, directing HR enterprises, or aligning HR strategies with organizational goals.

2. Exam Pattern: SHRM-CP &SCP

2. EXAM PATTERN OF SHRM -CP & SCP CERTIFICATION

SHRM -CP Exam Format

- The SHRM-CP exam includes two types of multiple-choice questions:
  - Stand-alone knowledge-based items evaluate factual information comprehension.
  - Scenario-based situational judgment items assess judgment and decision-making skills.
- Roughly half of the exam items are distributed across three behavioral competency clusters.
- The remaining half are allocated across three HR knowledge domains.

Content and Structure:

- The SHRM-CP exam consists of 134 multiple-choice questions.
- Among these, 24 questions are unscored, serving SHRM's evaluation purposes.
- The exam duration is 3 hours and 40 minutes.

Question Types:

There are two types of multiple-choice questions: knowledge-based (KI and FKI) and situational judgment questions (SJI)

Knowledge Questions:

- KIs relate to the 14 HR functional areas, while FKIs cover the 9 behavioral competencies.

Situational Judgment Questions:

- SJIs assess decision-making skills by presenting work-related scenarios.

Question Grouping:

- Questions are divided into two groups: behavioral competencies and technical competencies.

SHRM-CP Exam Registration:

Application Process:

- Create an online SHRM account and apply to register for the exam.
- Pay the applicable examination fee with the application based on the submission timeline.

Examination Fees:

Submission Timeline	SHRM Member Fee	Non-member Fee
Early Bird	$300	$400
Standard	$375	$475
Military	$270	$270
Student	$149	$209

Authorization to Test (ATT):

- Upon approval of the application and fee, receive an ATT detailing exam scheduling instructions.

Test Day:

In-person Testing:

- Arrive 15 to 30 minutes before the scheduled exam time.
- Present a valid, government-issued ID and sign a candidate agreement.
- Store personal items in provided lockers outside the testing.
- One 15-minute break is permitted during the exam.

Live Remote Proctoring:

- Log in to your account 15 to 30 minutes before the testing appointment.

- Display a valid photo ID and scan the testing environment for compliance.
- The proctor enables the launch button upon readiness.
- Maintain visibility of hands and stay in front of the camera throughout the exam.
- One 15-minute break is allowed during the test.

Tips to Pass the SHRM Exam:

Effective Study Methods:

- Regularly evaluate progress using practice tests.
- Focus on areas of weakness identified through practice tests.

Understanding Answer Explanations:

- Investigate every concept related to questions, ensuring thorough understanding.

Comprehensive Topic Comprehension:

- Memorization of practice questions is insufficient.
- Fully understand concepts to tackle any question on the exam.

Strategy for Practice:

- Begin with no time constraints, gradually introduce time limits, and simulate test day conditions.
- Regular practice builds readiness for the exam environment and enhances recall of learned material.

Other Queries

Duration of Exam:

- The SHRM-CP exam has a time limit of 3 hours and 40 minutes.

Number of Questions:

- There are 134 multiple-choice questions on the SHRM-CP exam, including 24 unscored.

Difficulty Level:

- The SHRM-CP exam is moderately complex and requires thorough preparation to pass.

SHRM CP/SCP Exam Scoring

Raw Score vs. Scaled Score:

- Based on correct answers, you receive a raw score (0-110), but your reported score is scaled (120-200).
- 200 is the passing score (achieves competency level).

Score Report:

- Provides feedback on performance across competency clusters and knowledge domains.
- Helps unsuccessful candidates assess their weaknesses for future attempts.
- Guides successful candidates in recertification and development.

Equating:

- Statistical process adjusts scores for exam form difficulty variations.
- Ensures fairness across different exam versions.

Pass/Fail Basis:
- Exams are not "curved" - everyone meeting standards passes.
- Focuses on individual competency achievement.

SHRM-CP Exam Composition:

Topic Area	Percentage
Organization	18%
People	18%
Leadership	17%
Business	16.5%
Interpersonal	16.5%
Workplace	14%

Additionally, there are 24 field-test items randomly mixed with scored exam items to gather data on question effectiveness, which do not count toward a candidate's score.

SHRM-CP Exam Question Types :

Question Type	Percentage	Statement
HR Specific Knowledge	50%	Key Concepts & Topics related to HR Functional Areas
Situational Judgement	40%	Choose the best strategy to address issues given in a work-related scenario
Leadership (Behavioral Competencies)	10%	Key Foundational Topics related to behavioral competencies

SHRM -SCP Exam Format

- Exam duration: Four hours, including 3 and 40 minutes of testing time.

- Total questions: 134, comprising 80 knowledge items and 54 situational-judgment items.

- Field-test items: 24 of the situational-judgment items are field-test items.
- Testing format: Computer-based testing.

- Exam options: Available for in-person testing at authorized testing centers or via live remote proctoring from home.

SHRM-SCP Exam Composition:

Topic Area	Percentage
Organization	18%
People	18%
Leadership	17%
Business	16.5%
Interpersonal	16.5%
Workplace	14%

SHRM-SCP Exam Question Types :

Question Type	Percentage	Statement
HR Specific Knowledge	50%	Key Concepts & Topics related to HR Functional Areas
Situational Judgement	40%	Choose the best strategy to address issues given in a work-related scenario
Leadership (Behavioral Competencies)	10%	Key Foundational Topics related to behavioral competencies

Understanding Proficiency Indicators:

- Define competent HR behavior and performance.

- Both sets apply to all HR professionals, including senior and executive levels.

- HR executives must understand concepts, recognize strategic importance, and mentor junior employees.

- Crucial for HR professionals preparing for the **SHRM-SCP** exam to consider.

3. Behavioral Competencies- Leadership Cluster

9 Behavioral Competencies

Leadership Cluster	Interpersonal Cluster	Business Cluster
Leadership and Navigation	Relationship Management	Business Acumen
Ethical Practice	Communication	Consultation
Diversity, Equity, and Inclusion	Global Mindset	Analytical Aptitude

(A) Leadership Cluster

Behavioral Competency (1) Leadership and Navigation

- **Definition**: Knowledge, skills, abilities, and characteristics *(KSAOs).*

- **Purpose**: Create a compelling vision and mission for HR.

- **Alignment**: Align with the organization's strategic direction and culture.

- **Goals**: Accomplish HR and organizational goals.

- **Change Management**: Lead and promote organizational change.

- **Organization Navigation**: Navigate the organization effectively.

- **Initiative Management**: Manage implementation and execution of HR initiatives.

Key Concept: Leadership Theories

Leadership Theory	Definition	Example
Situational Leadership	Leadership style that adapts based on the situation and the readiness or maturity of followers.	A manager adjusts their leadership approach based on the experience and skill level of their team.
Transformational Leadership	Focuses on inspiring and motivating followers to achieve higher levels of performance and create meaningful changes.	A CEO who inspires employees to embrace a new company vision and achieve ambitious goals.
Participative Leadership	Involves sharing decision-making authority with group members to encourage their involvement and commitment.	A team leader involves team members in the decision-making process to boost morale and motivation.
Inclusive Leadership	Emphasizes creating an environment where all team members feel valued, respected, and included in decision-making.	A manager fosters diversity and inclusion within the team, ensuring everyone's voice is heard.
Leader-Member Exchange Theory	Focuses on the quality of relationships between leaders and individual followers, emphasizing mutual trust and respect.	A supervisor builds strong relationships with each team member, leading to higher job satisfaction and performance.
Servant Leadership	Emphasizes serving others' needs, prioritizing their growth and well-being, and empowering them to reach their potential.	A leader focuses on supporting and developing their team members, putting their needs first.
Transactional Leadership	Involves setting clear expectations and providing rewards or consequences based on performance.	A manager offers bonuses to employees who meet or exceed their targets, creating a culture of accountability.
Trait Theory	Focuses on identifying inherent characteristics or traits that distinguish effective leaders from non-leaders.	An organization assesses potential leaders based on traits such as confidence, empathy, and integrity.
Contingency Theory	Proposes that the effectiveness of a leader depends on various situational factors, such as the task, team, and environment.	A manager adapts their leadership style based on the specific challenges and circumstances they face.

Key Concept: People Management Technique

People Management Technique	Definition	Example
Coaching	Involves guiding and developing employees to improve their performance, skills, and abilities through feedback and guidance.	A manager provides regular one-on-one coaching sessions to help employees enhance their skills and achieve their goals.
Supporting	Entails providing assistance, resources, and encouragement to employees to help them overcome challenges and achieve success.	A supervisor offers emotional support and resources to a team member experiencing difficulties at work or in their personal life.
Delegating	Involves assigning tasks and responsibilities to employees while providing them with the necessary authority and autonomy to complete them.	A team leader delegates project tasks to team members based on their strengths and expertise, empowering them to take ownership.
Mentoring	Involves pairing a more experienced individual (mentor) with a less experienced individual (mentee) to provide guidance, support, and career advice.	A senior executive mentors a junior employee, offering insights, sharing experiences, and providing guidance

Key Concept : Motivational Theories

Motivation Theory	Definition	Example
Goal-Setting Theory	Focuses on setting specific, challenging goals that lead to higher performance and motivation when achieved.	An organization sets clear performance goals for employees, driving them to work harder and achieve desired outcomes.
Expectancy Theory	Proposes that individuals are motivated to act when they believe their efforts will lead to desired performance outcomes.	An employee is motivated to work hard because they believe their efforts will result in a promotion or salary increase.
Attribution Theory	Examines how individuals attribute success or failure to internal or external factors, influencing their motivation.	An employee attributes their promotion to their hard work and dedication, enhancing their motivation to perform well.
Self-Determination Theory	Focuses on intrinsic motivation and autonomy, suggesting that individuals are motivated when they feel in control of their actions and decisions.	An employee is motivated because they enjoy their work and feel a sense of autonomy in completing tasks.
Equity Theory	Examines how individuals perceive fairness in the distribution of rewards and resources, impacting their motivation.	An employee becomes demotivated when they perceive that their coworker receives higher pay for the same level of work.
Herzberg's 2-Factor Theory	Distinguishes between hygiene factors (job context) and motivators (job content) to understand factors influencing motivation and job satisfaction.	An employee is motivated by opportunities for growth and recognition, while dissatisfaction arises from poor working conditions.

Key Concept: Influence and persuasion techniques

Influence and Persuasion Technique	Definition	Example
Personal Appeal	Involves appealing to personal interests, values, or emotions to persuade others to take a desired action.	An HR manager convinces employees to participate in a wellness program by highlighting the personal health benefits.
Forming Coalitions	Involves building alliances or partnerships with individuals or groups to influence decisions or outcomes collectively.	An HR team collaborates with other departments to advocate for changes in company policies or procedures.
Leading by Example	Involves demonstrating desired behaviors or actions to inspire others to follow suit and adopt similar practices.	A senior HR leader models ethical behavior and professionalism, influencing junior staff to emulate their conduct.
Rational Persuasion	Involves presenting logical arguments, evidence, or data to persuade others to adopt a particular course of action.	An HR professional persuades company executives to invest in employee training by demonstrating its positive impact on performance and productivity.

Key Concept: Personal leadership qualities

Personal Leadership Qualities	Definition	Example
Vision	Involves having a clear and inspiring picture of the future and the ability to articulate it to motivate and guide others.	A CEO communicates a compelling vision for the company's future, inspiring employees to work towards common goals.
Self-Motivation	Involves the ability to drive oneself towards achieving goals and overcoming obstacles without external influence or supervision.	An HR manager maintains high levels of motivation to meet project deadlines and exceed performance expectations.
Self-Discipline	Involves the ability to control one's impulses, emotions, and actions, staying focused on goals and maintaining consistency in behavior.	A team leader adheres to a strict schedule and follows through on commitments, setting an example for team members.
Risk Taking	Involves the willingness to take calculated risks and explore new opportunities to achieve personal or organizational growth.	An HR director implements innovative HR practices, taking calculated risks to improve employee engagement and retention.
Commitment to Continuous Learning	Involves the dedication to ongoing personal and professional development, seeking out new knowledge and skills to stay relevant and effective.	A training manager regularly attends workshops and conferences to stay updated on industry trends and best practices.
Growth Mindset	Involves the belief that abilities and intelligence can be developed through effort and perseverance, leading to resilience and a desire for learning.	An HR consultant embraces challenges as opportunities for growth, viewing setbacks as temporary and focusing on improvement.

Subcompetencies of Leadership & Navigation

(A) Navigating the Organization

Master these skills to demonstrate proficiency in navigating your organization for successful HR initiatives:

Understanding Formal & Informal Dynamics:

- **Formal**: Know the organizational hierarchy, reporting structures, and official roles.
- **Informal**: Be aware of unofficial power dynamics, key influencers, and relationships within the organization.
- **Leader Goals & Interests**: Understand the priorities and motivations of key leaders to align HR initiatives accordingly.

Facilitating Communication & Decision-Making:

- **Bridge the Gap**: Foster communication between departments and levels to ensure everyone is informed and involved in HR initiatives.
- **Empower Decision-Making**: Create a collaborative environment where stakeholders can contribute and participate in decision-making processes related to HR initiatives.

Leveraging Organizational Culture & Politics:

- **Cultural Awareness**: Be attuned to the organization's values, beliefs, and assumptions to ensure HR initiatives resonate with the workforce.
- **Political Savvy**: Navigate the organization's political landscape effectively. Understand how decisions are made and who holds influence, and use this knowledge to advocate for HR initiatives.

Utilizing Structure & Systems:

- **Understanding Systems & Processes:** Grasp the key HR processes, systems, and policies relevant to your initiatives.

- **Streamlined Implementation:** Leverage existing systems and processes to facilitate the successful implementation of HR initiatives with minimal disruption.

For Advanced HR Professionals:

- **Navigating Complex Relationships:** Understand the intricate connections and power dynamics between leaders to design, implement, and sustain HR initiatives effectively.

- **Strategic Influence:** Use your understanding of the organization's political environment to shape HR's strategic direction, manage change initiatives, and effectively address talent needs.

- **Optimizing Processes:** Analyze the complex web of formal and informal organizational processes, systems, and policies. Leverage this knowledge to develop and implement HR's strategic vision seamlessly.

(B) Vision

Master these points to demonstrate proficiency in defining and supporting a compelling HR vision:

For All HR Professionals:

Alignment with Organizational Strategy:

- Understand the business unit's and organization's culture, values, mission, and goals.
- Ensure your HR vision aligns with and supports these overarching objectives.

Actionable Goals:

- Define specific, measurable, achievable, relevant, and time-bound (SMART) goals for developing and implementing HR programs, practices, and policies.

Continuous Improvement:

- Proactively identify opportunities to improve HR operations to support better the strategic vision of both HR and the organization.

Vision Champion:

- Actively support implementing HR programs, practices, and policies that uphold the established strategic vision.

For Advanced HR Professionals (SHRM-SCP Focus):

Strategic Visionary:

- Go beyond the current state. Envision the ideal future state of the HR function, organization, and culture to identify areas for improvement.

Long-Term Planning:

- Develop a comprehensive long-term strategic direction, vision, and goals for HR and the organization. This plan should bridge the gap between the current and envisioned ideal future.

Communication & Collaboration:

- Create a comprehensive plan to achieve the strategic direction, vision, and goals.
- Actively solicit feedback from executive-level stakeholders on the proposed HR strategy and vision.

Adaptability:

- Be prepared to adjust the HR strategy, approaches, and programs in response to significant internal or external changes that might impact the organization's goals.

(C) Managing HR Initiatives

Master these skills to implement and support successful HR projects effectively:

For All HR Professionals:

- **Project Clarity**: Clearly define and elaborate on project requirements set by leadership. Ensure everyone involved understands the project's goals and scope.

Goal Setting & Monitoring:

- Establish clear, measurable project goals and progress milestones.
- Regularly monitor progress to ensure the project stays on track and meets deadlines.

Resource Management:

- Develop and manage project budgets effectively, allocating resources efficiently.
- Identify and monitor the resources necessary for successful project implementation and ongoing maintenance.
- Be prepared to adjust resource allocation if needed to meet project demands.

Problem-Solving & Adaptability:

- Proactively identify potential obstacles that could hinder project success.
- Develop solutions to overcome these challenges and ensure project completion.
- Demonstrate agility and adaptability when project requirements, goals, or constraints change.

For Advanced HR Professionals (SHRM-SCP Focus):

- **Strategic Translation:** Bridge the gap between vision and action. Translate HR's vision, strategic direction, and long-term goals into specific, actionable projects and initiatives with clear timelines and goals.

- **Vision Alignment:** Continuously monitor the progress of HR initiatives to ensure they align with and contribute to achieving HR's overall vision, strategic direction, and long-term goals.

- **Collaborative Leadership:** Actively collaborate with leadership to identify and remove obstacles to the successful implementation of HR initiatives.

- **Resource Optimization:** Obtain and deploy necessary organizational resources to support HR initiatives effectively. Monitor their effectiveness and adjust as needed to ensure optimal utilization.

- **Accountability Champion:** Foster a culture of accountability within the HR team. Ensure clear ownership and responsibility for successfully implementing project plans and initiatives.

(D) Influence

Master these skills to become a persuasive force for HR initiatives:

For All HR Professionals:

- **HR Credibility**: Establish yourself as a trusted HR expert internally and externally among stakeholders.
- **Building Buy-In**: Secure the support of key stakeholders (leaders, employees) for HR initiatives. Communicate the value proposition of HR programs and demonstrate how they align with organizational goals.
- **Motivational Leader**: Inspire and motivate HR staff and other stakeholders to support HR's vision and goals.
- **Strategic Advocacy**: Champion the organization's strategic direction and goals, advocating for the organization and its employees.

- **Courageous Communication:** Share your opinions about important HR issues, even if they differ from prevailing views. Don't be discouraged by potential pushback.

For Advanced HR Professionals (SHRM-SCP Focus):

- **HR Champion:** Proactively promote the HR function's critical role in achieving the organization's overall mission, vision, and goals.

- **Expanded Credibility:** Establish yourself as a recognized HR expert beyond the organization, potentially at a regional, national, or even international level.

- **Influential Voice:** Become a powerful advocate for HR strategies, philosophies, and initiatives within the organization.

- **Evidence-Based Advocacy:** Champion the implementation of HR solutions supported by solid data and research (evidence-based practices).

- **Inspiring All Levels:** Motivate HR staff, non-HR personnel, and executive-level stakeholders to embrace and actively pursue the organization's strategic direction, vision, and long-term goals.

- **Consensus Builder:** Facilitate discussions and collaboration among leaders to build consensus on the organization's strategic direction and long-term goals.

- **Strategic Influence:** Leverage your HR knowledge and expertise to influence the organization's overall business strategy, ensuring HR plays a vital role in organizational decision-making.

- **Empowering Environment:** Promote a work environment where calculated risk-taking is encouraged, and employees feel comfortable sharing ideas, fostering innovation within the organization.

Quiz Corner 1- Leadership and Navigation

Stand-alone Knowledge-Based Questions:

1) Which leadership theory focuses on setting specific, challenging goals to enhance performance?

A) Transformational Leadership
B) Situational Leadership
C) Goal-Setting Theory
D) Servant Leadership

2) Which people management technique involves assigning tasks and responsibilities while giving employees authority and autonomy?

A) Delegating
B) Coaching
C) Supporting
D) Mentoring

3) Which motivational theory proposes that individuals are motivated when they believe their efforts will lead to desired performance outcomes?

A) Equity Theory
B) Self-Determination Theory
C) Expectancy Theory
D) Attribution Theory

4) Which influence and persuasion technique involves appealing to personal interests, values, or emotions to persuade others?

A) Forming Coalitions
B) Leading by Example
C) Rational Persuasion
D) Personal Appeal

Quiz Corner 1- Leadership and Navigation

5) Which personal leadership quality involves having a clear and inspiring picture of the future?

A) Vision
B) Self-Motivation
C) Risk Taking
D) Growth Mindset

Scenario-Based Situational Judgment Items:

6) Scenario: As an HR manager, you notice a declining employee morale. Which leadership theory would you apply to inspire and motivate employees toward improved performance?

A) Transformational Leadership
B) Situational Leadership
C) Goal-Setting Theory
D) Servant Leadership

7) Scenario: Your team is having trouble meeting project deadlines. Which people management technique would you employ to empower them to overcome obstacles?

A) Delegating
B) Coaching
C) Supporting
D) Mentoring

8) Scenario: Some employees are reluctant to embrace changes in organizational policies. Which motivational theory would you apply to encourage their acceptance and adaptation?

A) Equity Theory
B) Self-Determination Theory
C) Expectancy Theory
D) Attribution Theory

Quiz Corner 1- Leadership and Navigation

9) Scenario: You must persuade a team member to undertake a new project. Which influence and persuasion technique would you use to motivate them?

A) Forming Coalitions
B) Leading by Example
C) Rational Persuasion
D) Personal Appeal

10) Scenario: Maintaining a positive outlook is crucial for team morale amid organizational changes. Which personal leadership quality would you demonstrate to inspire confidence and optimism?

A) Vision
B) Self-Motivation
C) Risk Taking
D) Growth Mindset

ANSWERS: Quiz Corner 1- Leadership and Navigation

1. Correct Answer: C) Goal-Setting Theory

2. Correct Answer: A) Delegating

3. Correct Answer: C) Expectancy Theory

4. Correct Answer: D) Personal Appeal

5. Correct Answer: A) Vision

6. Correct Answer: A) Transformational Leadership
Explanation: *Transformational leadership inspires and motivates employees by creating a compelling vision for the future and fostering a shared purpose. This approach would most effectively address declining morale by giving employees direction and motivation to work towards common goals.*

ANSWERS: Quiz Corner 1- Leadership and Navigation

7. Correct Answer: A) Delegating
Explanation: Delegating involves assigning tasks and responsibilities while giving employees the authority and autonomy to accomplish them. By delegating tasks effectively, you empower your team members to take ownership of their work and overcome challenges, enhancing productivity and meeting project deadlines.

8. Correct Answer: B) Self-Determination Theory
Explanation: Self-determination theory focuses on intrinsic motivation and autonomy, suggesting that individuals are motivated when they feel in control of their actions and decisions. Applying this theory would involve providing employees with opportunities for autonomy and involvement in the change process, empowering them to embrace and adapt to organizational changes more willingly.

9. Correct Answer: D) Personal Appeal
Explanation: Personal Appeal involves appealing to personal interests, values, or emotions to persuade others. In this scenario, using a personal appeal would involve highlighting how the new project aligns with the team member's interests, goals, or values, motivating them to take on the challenge.

10. Correct Answer: D) Growth Mindset
Explanation: A Growth Mindset involves believing that abilities and intelligence can be developed through effort and perseverance. Demonstrating a Growth Mindset would involve viewing organizational changes as opportunities for learning and development, inspiring confidence and optimism among team members.

(A) Leadership Cluster
Behavioral Competency (2): Ethical Practice

Ethical Practice encompasses the knowledge, skills, abilities, and other characteristics (KSAOs) required to maintain high levels of personal and professional integrity, adhere to ethical business principles and practices and act as an ethical agent promoting core values, integrity, and accountability throughout the organization.

Key Concept: Ethical business principles and practices

Principle	Definition	Example (SHRM Exam Focus)
Transparency	Conducting oneself in a way that is open, honest, and accountable.	Disclosing all relevant information to stakeholders, even if it's unfavorable. (e.g., Informing employees about a necessary downsizing while also providing outplacement services and severance packages).
Authenticity	Being genuine and true to oneself and one's values.	Avoiding misrepresentation of facts or qualifications during the hiring process. (e.g., Being upfront with a candidate about the specific requirements of a role and not exaggerating the potential for advancement).
Conflicts of Interest	Avoiding situations where personal interests could influence professional judgment.	Disclosing potential conflicts and recusing oneself from decision-making processes when necessary. (e.g., An HR professional steps aside from participating in the hiring process for a relative or close friend).
Integrity	Upholding ethical standards and acting with honesty and fairness.	Ensuring fair and unbiased treatment of all employees during performance evaluations and promotion opportunities.
Accountability	Taking ownership of one's actions and decisions.	Taking responsibility for mistakes and proactively seeking solutions to rectify them. (e.g., Acknowledging an error in a new policy rollout and working with stakeholders to implement necessary corrections).
Promoting Core Values	Actively advocating for the organization's core ethical principles.	Encouraging employees to report unethical behavior through anonymous reporting channels.

Key Concept: Privacy Principles and Policies

Privacy principles and policies encompass the knowledge, skills, abilities, and other characteristics (KSAOs) required to establish and uphold privacy standards, safeguard sensitive information, and ensure compliance with relevant regulations and guidelines.

Principle	Definition	Example (SHRM Exam Focus)
Anonymity	Ensuring that individuals' identities are protected and not readily identifiable.	Implementing anonymous surveys to gather feedback from employees on sensitive topics such as workplace culture or harassment.
Confidentiality	Safeguarding sensitive information and restricting access to authorized individuals.	Maintaining confidentiality when handling employee medical records or disciplinary actions.
Opt-in/Opt-out Policies	Providing individuals with the choice to participate (opt-in) or decline participation (opt-out) in certain activities or data collection processes.	Allowing employees to opt-out of sharing personal information for marketing purposes within the organization's intranet.

Key Concept: Internal Ethics Controls

Internal ethics controls involve the knowledge, skills, abilities, and other characteristics (KSAOs) necessary to establish and maintain ethical standards within an organization, including protecting employee confidentiality and implementing standards for employee investigations.

Principle	Definition	Example (SHRM Exam Focus)
Protection of Employee Confidentiality	Ensuring the privacy and confidentiality of employee information, including personal and sensitive data, in accordance with legal and organizational guidelines.	Implementing secure data storage systems and access controls to prevent unauthorized disclosure of employee information.
Standards for Employee Investigations	Establishing and adhering to procedures and protocols for conducting fair, thorough, and impartial investigations into employee misconduct or grievances.	Following a standardized investigation process, including interviewing witnesses, collecting evidence, and documenting findings.

Sub-Competency:

(A) Personal Integrity

Core Principles (For All HR Professionals):

Value Alignment (Walk the Talk):

- **Definition:** Your actions consistently reflect your stated values and the organization's ethical principles.
- **SHRM-CP Example:** Upholding confidentiality of employee information even when pressured by colleagues.

Accountability (Owning Your Actions):

- **Definition:** Taking responsibility for mistakes and implementing solutions to rectify them.
- **SHRM-CP Example:** Acknowledging errors in HR processes and proposing revisions to ensure fair treatment of employees.

Self-Awareness (Recognizing Biases):

- **Definition:** Identifying both explicit and unconscious biases within yourself and others and actively working to mitigate their impact.
- **SHRM-CP Example:** Recognizing potential bias in talent acquisition practices and implementing strategies for fairer hiring (e.g., standardized interview questions, diverse interview panels).

Role Modeling (Setting the Standard):

- **Definition:** Exemplifying high ethical standards in all HR interactions, fostering trust with employees and colleagues.
- **SHRM-CP Example:** Treating everyone with respect and courtesy, regardless of their position or role in the organization.

Advanced Focus for SHRM-SCP:

The SHRM-SCP exam expects a higher level of leadership and initiative regarding personal integrity. Here's how the focus expands:

Conflict Management:
- **Definition:** Proactively address potential conflicts of interest or unethical behavior by escalating concerns to appropriate authorities.
- **SHRM-SCP Example:** Bringing potential favoritism in promotions to the attention of senior leadership.

Promoting Bias Awareness:
- **Definition:** Educate others within the organization about implicit bias and its influence on decision-making, fostering inclusive practices.
- **SHRM-SCP Example:** Conducting workshops for managers and HR professionals on recognizing and mitigating unconscious bias.

Enforcing Accountability:
- **Definition:** Hold colleagues accountable for their commitments by following established reporting procedures when unethical behavior is observed.
- **SHRM-SCP Example:** Addressing a colleague's unethical conduct by reporting it to the appropriate supervisor or HR department.

Sub-Competency: (B) Professional Integrity

For All HR Professionals

Key Behavior	Description
Confidentiality & Legal Compliance	Maintain confidentiality of sensitive employee information as required by law and professional ethics. Comply with legal mandates to report unethical behavior within the organization.
Discretion in Communication	Use sound judgment when communicating sensitive information, balancing transparency with confidentiality needs. Inform stakeholders about potential limitations of confidentiality and privacy.
Staying Current on Ethics	Proactively maintain your knowledge of ethical laws, standards, and emerging trends that might impact HR practices.
Fair and Thorough Investigations	Conduct HR investigations objectively, thoroughly, and in a timely manner, ensuring impartiality.
Building Credibility & Trust	Establish yourself as a reliable and trustworthy HR professional through your actions and interactions.
Decision-Making Without Bias	Avoid letting personal biases influence your professional decisions. Make choices based on fairness and ethical principles.
Upholding Ethical Standards	Apply the organization's ethics and integrity policies while actively challenging practices that may raise ethical concerns.
Navigating Political & Social Pressures	Manage political and social pressures effectively when making HR decisions and implementing HR initiatives.
Providing Ethical Feedback	Offer open, honest, and constructive feedback to colleagues whenever ethical issues arise.
Balancing Act	Strive for a balance between ethics, integrity, organizational success, employee advocacy, legal requirements, and organizational policies.
Continuous Learning	Actively seek opportunities to learn new skills and enhance existing ones to excel as an HR professional.

Sub-Competency: (B) Professional Integrity

For for Advanced HR Professionals (SHRM-SCP Focus)

Key Behavior	Description
Resisting Political Influence	Withstand undue political pressure during strategy development, initiative implementation, and long-term goal setting.
Ethical Strategic Balance	Balance ethics, integrity, organizational success, employee advocacy, and organizational mission and values when creating HR strategy, initiatives, and long-term goals.
Building HR Team Credibility	Foster trust and credibility for the HR team within the organization, becoming a go-to resource for ethical guidance.
Ethical Business Alignment	Champion the alignment of HR and business practices with prevailing ethical laws and standards.
Tough Ethical Decisions	Make difficult decisions that uphold the organization's values and maintain ethical integrity.
Responsible Use of Authority	Utilize power and authority appropriately, avoiding personal gain or favoritism.
Ethical Courage	Demonstrate agility and courage when making challenging decisions or navigating complex ethical situations.

Sub-Competency: (C) Ethical Agent

For All HR Professionals

Proficiency Indicator	Description
Empowers Reporting of Unethical Behaviors	Empowers all employees to report unethical behaviors and conflicts of interest without fear of reprisal.
Mitigates Bias in HR and Business Decisions	Takes steps to mitigate the influence of bias in HR and business decisions.
Maintains Transparency in HR Programs	Maintains appropriate levels of transparency for HR programs, practices, and policies.
Identifies and Communicates Ethical Risks	Identifies, evaluates, and communicates to leadership potential ethical risks and conflicts of interest.
Ensures Staff Access to Ethical Standards	Ensures staff members have access to and understand the organization's ethical standards and policies.

Sub-Competency: (C) Ethical Agent

For Advanced HR Professionals

Proficiency Indicator	Description
Advises Senior Management of Organizational Risks	Advises senior management of organizational risks and conflicts of interest.
Supports Internal Ethics Controls	Collaborates with leaders to support internal ethics controls.
Develops Expertise for HR Policies and Standards	Develops and provides expertise for HR policies, standards, and other internal ethics controls to minimize organizational risks from unethical practices.
Oversees HR Programs Driving Ethical Culture	Creates and oversees HR programs, practices, and policies that drive an ethical culture, encourage employees to report unethical behaviors, and protect the confidentiality of employees and data.
Communicates Vision for Consistent Organizational Values	Communicates a vision for an organizational culture in which there is consistency between the organization's stated and enacted values.
Designs High Standard Ethics Programs	Develops HR programs, practices, and policies that meet high standards of ethics and integrity.
Ensures Thorough, Timely, and Impartial Investigations	Designs and oversees systems to ensure that all investigations are conducted in a thorough, timely, and impartial manner.
Audits Adherence to HR Ethics Programs	Audits and monitors adherence to HR programs, practices, and policies pertaining to ethics.
Designs Learning Programs Covering Ethics	Designs and oversees learning and development programs covering ethics.
Implements Culture Encouraging Reporting	Implements and maintains a culture and system that encourages all employees to report unethical practices and behaviors.

Quiz Corner 2 - Ethical Practice

Stand-alone Knowledge-Based Questions:

1. Which of the following best describes the concept of authenticity in the context of ethical leadership?

a) Following trends and popular leadership styles.
b) Leading by example and acting in accordance with stated values.
c) Prioritizing personal gain and career advancement over employee well-being.
d) Adapting leadership style based on the situation without clear principles.

2) An organization implements a new policy requiring employees to report potential conflicts of interest. What is the primary purpose of such a policy?

a) To restrict employee interactions with external parties.
b) To identify and mitigate situations that could compromise ethical decision-making.
c) To punish employees who engage in unethical behavior.
d) To limit employee access to confidential company information.

3) What is an example of an internal ethics control mechanism within an organization?

a) Government regulations on workplace discrimination.
b) An organization's code of ethics and conduct.
c) Industry best practices for a specific job role.
d) Professional codes of conduct for HR professionals.

4) What is the critical difference between confidentiality and anonymity in the context of reporting unethical behavior?

a) Confidentiality protects the whistleblower's identity, while anonymity does not.
b) Anonymity protects the whistleblower's identity, while confidentiality protects the reported party.
c) There is no difference; they are interchangeable terms.
d) Confidentiality applies to all employee information, while anonymity applies only to specific reports.

Quiz Corner 2- Ethical Practice

5) An organization is revising its HR policies to promote a more ethical work environment. Which of the following elements would be MOST beneficial to include?

a) Detailed descriptions of specific penalties for ethical violations.
b) Clear and accessible channels for reporting unethical behavior.
c) A complex reward system for employees who consistently demonstrate ethical conduct.
d) Limited access to information on the organization's ethical code and policies.

Scenario-Based Situational Judgment Items:

6) You receive an anonymous report alleging a supervisor is misusing company funds. How would you approach this situation to ensure a fair investigation while protecting the whistleblower?

a) Immediately confront the supervisor and demand an explanation.
b) Dismiss the report as potentially unfounded without further investigation.
c) Disclose the whistleblower's identity to ensure a more thorough investigation.
d) Maintain confidentiality of the whistleblower and initiate a discreet investigation.

7) During a performance review, an employee expresses concern about the organization sharing too much personal information about employees on the company intranet. The information is not confidential but includes details about hobbies and family life. How would you address this concern?

a) Explain the importance of transparency and dismiss the employee's concerns.
b) Review the intranet content and remove any information deemed overly personal.
c) Ignore the employee's concerns, as this information is not technically confidential.
d) Encourage the employee to file a complaint against the organization formally.

Quiz Corner 2- Ethical Practice

8) You are tasked with developing a training program to raise employee awareness of ethical conduct within the organization. What key elements would you incorporate into this program to cultivate a robust ethical climate?

a) Focus solely on the legal consequences of unethical behavior.
b) Incorporate real-world scenarios and case studies to illustrate ethical dilemmas.
c) Present the organization's code of ethics as a lengthy and complex document.
d) Emphasize the importance of blind obedience to authority figures.

9) A manager asks you to help them downplay the severity of a workplace safety incident to avoid negative publicity. This action would violate the organization's commitment to transparency. What is the most appropriate course of action?

a) Agree to help the manager to protect the organization's reputation.
b) Ignore the request and hope the incident goes unreported.
c) Politely but firmly decline the manager's request and explain the importance of transparency.
d) Threaten to report the manager to their superiors if they don't downplay the incident.

10) The organization is implementing a new HR policy restricting employee access to social media during work hours. While this policy aims to improve productivity, some employees express concerns about micromanagement. How can you address these concerns while ensuring adherence to the new policy?

a) Ignore employee concerns and strictly enforce the new policy.
b) Allow unrestricted access to social media and trust employees to manage their time effectively.
c) Develop clear guidelines for acceptable use of social media during work hours.
d) Scrap the new policy altogether due to employee concerns about micromanagement.

ANSWERS: Quiz Corner 2- Ethical Practice

1. The answer is b) Leading by example and acting in accordance with stated values.
2. The answer is b) To identify and mitigate situations that could compromise ethical decision-making.
3. The answer is b) An organization's code of ethics and conduct.
4. The answer is a) Confidentiality protects the whistleblower's identity, while anonymity does not.
5. The answer is b) Clear and accessible channels for reporting unethical behavior.
6. The answer is d) Maintain confidentiality of the whistleblower and initiate a discreet investigation.

Explanation: Protecting the whistleblower's anonymity is crucial to encourage future reports of unethical behavior. Initiating a discreet investigation allows gathering evidence without tipping off the accused supervisor.

7. Answer: B) Review the intranet content and remove any information deemed overly personal.

Explanation: Balancing privacy with transparency is essential. While the information may not be strictly confidential, respecting employee privacy concerns fosters trust and demonstrates respect for boundaries. Reviewing and removing overly personal details shows responsiveness to employee feedback.

8. The answer is b) Incorporate real-world scenarios and case studies to illustrate ethical dilemmas.

Explanation: Using real-world examples helps employees understand how ethical principles apply to everyday work situations. Discussing case studies allows interactive learning and encourages critical thinking about ethical decision-making.

9. The answer is c) Politely but firmly decline the manager's request and explain the importance of transparency.

Explanation: Upholding ethical principles takes priority over protecting the organization's image. Transparency is crucial for maintaining trust and ensuring a safe work environment.

10. The answer is c) Develop clear guidelines for acceptable use of social media during work hours.

Explanation: Finding a balance is critical. Providing clear guidelines for social media use during work hours addresses productivity concerns while alleviating employee concerns about micromanagement. Employees understand limitations while still having some level.

(A) Leadership Cluster
Behavioral Competency (3): Diversity, Equity & Inclusion

Diversity, Equity & Inclusion (DE&I) encompasses strategies to foster a work environment where individuals are treated fairly and respectfully, contributing fully to organizational success.

Key Concept	Description	Example (SHRM Exam Focus)
Characteristics of a Dynamic Workforce	Attributes representing diversity within a workforce, including multigenerational, multicultural, multilingual, multitalented, and multigendered components.	Multigenerational workforce with diverse skillsets.
Approaches to Developing an Inclusive Workplace	Tactics to cultivate inclusivity, such as executive sponsorship, allyship, and unconscious-bias training, aimed at fostering a sense of belonging.	Implementing allyship programs to promote inclusivity.
Workspace Solutions	Facilities and amenities provided to meet diverse workforce needs, like lactation rooms, prayer rooms, and gender-neutral restrooms, ensuring accessibility.	Installing gender-neutral restrooms for inclusivity.
Barriers to Success Involving Bias	Obstacles arising from conscious and unconscious biases, like gender-based discrimination, racism, stereotypes, and ageism, hindering career advancement.	Addressing gender-based discrimination in promotions.
Techniques to Measure and Increase Equity	Methods to assess and enhance equity, including diversity metrics, pay audits, and employee surveys, fostering fairness and transparency.	Conducting pay audits to ensure gender pay equity.
Benefits and Programs Supporting DE&I	Initiatives and offerings supporting diversity and inclusion, like caregiver options and workplace flexibility policies, enhancing organizational culture.	Offering paid leave options to support diverse families.
DE&I Metrics	Indicators measuring diversity, equity, and inclusion, like gender diversity and retention rates, assessing organizational inclusivity and equity effectiveness.	Analyzing retention rates for diverse employees.

Sub-competencies - Diversity, Equity & Inclusion

Theory: DE&I sub-competencies focus on fostering an inclusive culture, ensuring equity, and demonstrating the link between DE&I initiatives and organizational performance.

Sub-competency	Description
Creating a Diverse and Inclusive Culture	Establishing an environment where diverse individuals feel valued and included, fostering innovation and collaboration.
Ensuring Equity Effectiveness	Implementing fair policies and practices to mitigate biases and promote equal opportunities for all employees.
Connecting DE&I to Organizational Performance	Demonstrating how DE&I initiatives enhance organizational effectiveness, productivity, and employee engagement.

Sub competency (1): Creating a Diverse and Inclusive Culture

Proficiency Indicator	Example (SHRM Exam Focus)
Recognizes, supports, and advocates for a diverse workforce across various dimensions of diversity.	Advocating for inclusive hiring practices to ensure representation across race, gender, ethnicity, and abilities.
Identifies and implements workspace solutions to accommodate diverse needs.	Establishing lactation rooms and prayer spaces in the workplace to support employees' religious and caregiving needs.
Confronts and addresses bias, microaggressions, and acts of exclusion in the workplace.	Addressing instances of gender-based discrimination and subtle acts of exclusion during team meetings.
Provides professional development on cultural and diversity differences to employees at all levels.	Conducting workshops on cultural sensitivity and diversity awareness for both frontline staff and senior executives.
Communicates the benefits of DE&I initiatives to employees and leaders.	Highlighting how a diverse and inclusive workplace fosters innovation and enhances employee engagement.
Stays updated on current trends and best practices in DE&I management.	Attending conferences and webinars on DE&I strategies and incorporating latest research findings into HR practices.
Implements HR programs that encourage collaboration among diverse teams.	Initiating cross-functional projects to encourage collaboration among employees from different backgrounds.
Supports a workplace culture that encourages mutual respect and trust, and values diverse perspectives.	Establishing open-door policies and regular feedback sessions to foster an inclusive and supportive work environment.

For Advanced HR Professionals:

- Advocate for increased workforce diversity and inclusive practices.
- Partner with business leaders to develop enterprise-wide DE&I programs.
- Assess the organization's inclusiveness using DE&I metrics.
- Create policies fostering psychological safety and authentic expression.
- Promote allyship and courageous conversations around DE&I topics.

Sub competency (2) : Ensuring Equity Effectiveness

Ensures fair treatment in access, opportunity, and advancement for all individuals in the workplace.

Proficiency Indicator	Example (SHRM Exam Focus)
Contributes to developing an organizational culture that provides access, opportunity, and equity for all employees.	Collaborating with leadership to establish diversity and inclusion initiatives aimed at equitable opportunities for all.
Identifies and enhances the equity of organizational policies and procedures.	Reviewing recruitment processes to remove biases and ensure fair treatment for candidates from all backgrounds.
Assesses equity using tools to understand the relationship between empathy, inclusion, and behavior.	Conducting surveys or focus groups to gauge employees' perceptions of equity and inclusion within the organization.
Implements benefits and programs supporting a diverse and equitable workforce.	Introducing flexible work arrangements and childcare support to accommodate employees' diverse needs and situations.
Consults with managers on distinguishing between performance issues and DE&I differences.	Providing training to managers on addressing performance concerns while ensuring equitable treatment for all employees.
Partners with people managers to hire new employees from diverse groups.	Collaborating with hiring managers to ensure diverse candidate pools and unbiased selection processes.

For Advanced HR Professionals:

- Designs HR programs promoting an organizational culture of equity and access.
- Plans interventions to resolve identified inequities in policies and practices.
- Incorporates equity assessment results into HR strategy.
- Advocates for and oversees benefits supporting diversity and equity.
- Builds a diverse HR team and advises on empathetic and inclusive leadership behaviors.

Sub competency (3) : Connecting DE&I to Organizational Performance

Demonstrates the importance of DE&I efforts in achieving organizational goals and key objectives.

Proficiency Indicator	Example (SHRM Exam Focus)
Demonstrates support for the organization's DE&I efforts to internal and external stakeholders.	Participating in DE&I initiatives and promoting their importance during company meetings and external events.
Designs and executes effective DE&I initiatives aligned with business goals.	Developing mentorship programs aimed at fostering diversity and inclusion while enhancing leadership skills in employees.
Collects, analyzes, and communicates DE&I metric results to demonstrate their impact on organizational objectives.	Presenting data showing improvements in productivity and employee satisfaction as a result of DE&I initiatives.

For Advanced HR Professionals:

- Creates and advocates for the organizational business case for DE&I.
- Partners with leaders to integrate DE&I goals into the organization's strategic plan.
- Sets and monitors DE&I goals and metrics to measure their impact on organizational objectives.
- Integrates DE&I goals and best practices into all HR programs and policies.
- Identifies necessary changes related to DE&I in the workforce and workplace to support key business objectives.

Quiz Corner 3 - DIVERSITY, EQUITY & INCLUSION

Stand-alone Knowledge-Based Questions:

1. What are some characteristics of a dynamic workforce?

a) Limited experience and skillsets
b) Multigenerational; multicultural; multilingual; multitalented; multi-gendered
c) High turnover rate
d) Lack of innovation

2) Question: What is an example of a microaggression in the workplace?

a) Direct verbal assault based on someone's race.
b) A subtle comment or behavior that reinforces a stereotype about a group of people.
c) Openly discussing religious beliefs during a meeting.
d) Providing equal pay for equal work.

3) What is the primary purpose of unconscious bias training in the workplace?

a) To replace existing hiring practices.
b) To eliminate all forms of bias from employees.
c) To raise awareness of unconscious biases and their potential impact on decision-making.
d) To punish employees who exhibit biased behavior.

4) What is an example of a workplace benefit program that supports DE&I?

a) Standardized work schedule for all employees.
b) Caregiver options for employees with dependents.
c) Mandatory overtime policies.
d) Limited vacation time accrual.

Quiz Corner 3 - DIVERSITY, EQUITY & INCLUSION

5) What is an example of a DE&I metric used to assess an organization's progress?

- a) Employee satisfaction with company parties.
- b) Retention rates for employees from diverse backgrounds.
- c) Number of social media followers.
- d) Cost of employee training programs.

Scenario-Based Situational Judgment Items:

6) A seemingly qualified candidate stumbles slightly during a job interview while answering a question. You unconsciously associate this with a lack of confidence and begin to doubt their suitability for the role. How would you address this situation?

a) End the interview and move on to the next candidate.
b) Focus on the candidate's remaining answers and disregard the stumble.
c) Ask the candidate to repeat the question to confirm they understood it.
d) Casually inquire about the candidate's physical health during the interview.

7) A new employee from a different cultural background feels isolated and has difficulty connecting with colleagues. What steps can you take to promote a more inclusive work environment?

a) Advise the employee to adapt to the existing workplace culture.
b) Organize team-building activities that celebrate cultural diversity.
c) Assign the employee a mentor from their own cultural background.
d) Ignore the situation, assuming the employee will eventually adjust.

8) The organization is developing a new training program, but the materials are only available in English. Several employees from non-English speaking backgrounds express concern about their ability to participate. How would you address this concern?

a) Offer the training program on a voluntary basis.
b) Provide translated versions of the training materials or offer interpretation services.
c) All employees are required to complete the training regardless of language barriers.
d) Develop a shortened training program specifically for non-English speakers.

Quiz Corner 3 - DIVERSITY, EQUITY & INCLUSION

9) A business leader expresses skepticism about the value of DE&I initiatives, questioning their impact on the organization's bottom line. How would you respond?

a) Threaten to report the leader to HR for their discriminatory views.
b) Present personal anecdotes about the benefits of diversity.
c) Share data and research demonstrating the positive correlation between DE&I and organizational performance.
d) Ignore the leader's concerns and focus on implementing DE&I initiatives anyway.

10) You overhear a coworker making a seemingly offhand remark about a colleague's accent. While it might not be intended maliciously, you recognize it as a microaggression. How would you intervene in this situation?

a) Publicly confront the coworker and accuse them of racism.
b) Ignore the situation, assuming it's a minor issue.
c) Take your coworker aside and privately explain why the comment was insensitive.
d) Report the coworker to HR without any attempt to address the situation directly.

ANSWERS: Quiz Corner 3 - DIVERSITY, EQUITY & INCLUSION

1. b) Multigenerational; multicultural; multilingual; multitalented; multi-gendered
2. b) A subtle comment or behavior that reinforces a stereotype about a group of people.
3. c) To raise awareness of unconscious biases and their potential impact on decision-making.
4. b) Caregiver options for employees with dependents.
5. b) Retention rates for employees from diverse backgrounds.
6. Option b) is the most appropriate. Recognizing your potential bias, you should continue the interview, focusing on the candidate's qualifications and disregarding the stumble.

7. Answer: Option b) fosters inclusion by creating opportunities for cultural exchange and team bonding.

8. Option b) ensures equity by providing access to training materials in a format understandable to all employees. This could involve translated versions, subtitles, or interpretation services.

9. Option c) uses data-driven evidence to connect DE&I to business outcomes. This approach is more persuasive than emotional appeals or threats.

10. Option c) promotes a culture of respect by privately addressing the microaggression and raising awareness without creating unnecessary conflict.

4. Behavioral Competencies- Interpersonal Cluster

Interpersonal Cluster

Leadership Cluster	Interpersonal Cluster	Business Cluster
Leadership and Navigation	**Relationship Management**	Business Acumen
Ethical Practice	**Communication**	Consultation
Diversity, Equity, and Inclusion	**Global Mindset**	Analytical Aptitude

Interpersonal Cluster encompasses three key competencies crucial for HR professionals to function effectively in collaborative and interpersonal aspects of their roles:

Relationship Management:

- Building and maintaining professional networks.
- Fostering trust and rapport with colleagues.
- Collaborating effectively within teams.
- Negotiating mutually beneficial agreements.
- Managing conflict constructively.

Communication:

- Communicating clearly and concisely with diverse stakeholders.
- Actively listening and understanding different perspectives.
- Providing and receiving feedback effectively.
- Tailoring communication styles to different audiences.
- Utilizing various communication channels appropriately.

Global Mindset:

- Operating within a global workforce with sensitivity to cultural differences.
- Understanding global business practices and regulations.
- Promoting a culturally diverse and inclusive workplace.
- Adapting communication and leadership styles for international settings.
- Valuing the contributions of a multicultural workforce.

By mastering these competencies, HR professionals can build strong relationships, foster collaboration, and navigate the complexities of a diverse workplace environment.

(1) Relationship Management

Relationship Management encompasses the Knowledge, Skills, Abilities, and Other characteristics (KSAOs) necessary to establish and maintain professional networks within and outside the organization, nurture relationships, collaborate effectively in teams, negotiate mutually beneficial agreements, and manage conflicts while aligning with organizational objectives.

Sub-competencies:

A) Networking
B) Relationship Building
C) Teamwork
D) Negotiation
E) Conflict Management

Key Concepts:

Types of Conflict:

Conflict Type	Description	Examples
Relationship	Personal differences or interpersonal dynamics	Personality clashes, hurt feelings
Task	Disagreements over work methods, deadlines, priorities	Differing approaches to a project, missed deadlines
Interorganizational	Conflict between two or more organizations	Competition for resources, disagreements over contracts
Intraorganizational	Conflict within a team or department	Disagreements over strategy, communication issues

Conflict Resolution Strategies:

Strategy	Description	Examples
Accommodation	Yielding to the needs or interests of others	Agreeing to a coworker's proposal despite personal reservations
Collaboration	Working together to find a mutually acceptable solution	Brainstorming ideas with team members to address a common challenge
Compromise	Finding a middle ground where both parties make concessions	Adjusting project timelines to accommodate conflicting schedules
Competition	Pursuing one's own needs or interests at the expense of others	Advocating for personal objectives without considering team goals
Avoidance	Ignoring or postponing the conflict	Refusing to address disagreements in a team meeting

Negotiation Tactics, Strategies, and Styles:

Technique	Description	Example
Perspective Taking	Understanding the other party's needs and interests to find common ground	Listening actively to a coworker's concerns before proposing a solution
Principled Bargaining	Focusing on underlying interests rather than fixed positions	Exploring various options to meet both parties' needs
Auction	Competitive bidding process to determine the best offer	Soliciting proposals from multiple vendors to select a supplier
Interest-Based Bargaining	Seeking solutions that address the interests of both parties	Negotiating a contract with terms beneficial to both buyer and seller
Position-Based Bargaining	Holding firm to predetermined positions without exploring alternatives	Insisting on specific terms without considering alternative options

Trust-Building Techniques:

Technique	Description	Example
Emotional Intelligence	Understanding and managing emotions in oneself and others	Providing support to a colleague experiencing a personal challenge
Relatability	Finding common ground or shared experiences with others	Sharing personal anecdotes during team-building activities
Vulnerability	Being open and authentic about one's thoughts and feelings	Admitting mistakes and seeking feedback for improvement
Transparency	Being open and honest in communication and decision-making	Sharing information about organizational changes with employees
Recognizing Individual Strengths	Acknowledging and appreciating the unique contributions of each team member	Highlighting team members' achievements and strengths

Tips for the SHRM Exam:

- Understand the various types of conflict and appropriate resolution strategies for each.
- Familiarize yourself with negotiation tactics, strategies, and styles.
- Practice trust-building techniques such as active listening and transparency.
- Develop strong communication and interpersonal skills to navigate relationships effectively.
- By mastering these concepts and skills, you'll be well-prepared for the Relationship Management section of the SHRM CP/SCP exam and equipped to excel in your HR career.

Behavioral Competency - Relationship Management

Sub-Competency

(A) Networking

Definition: Networking involves establishing and cultivating professional relationships within and outside the organization, fostering connections that can be leveraged to achieve organizational goals.

Proficiency Indicators for All HR Professionals:

Internal Networking:

- Develops, maintains, and utilizes a network of professional contacts within the organization.
- Includes peers from HR and non-HR roles, HR customers, and stakeholders like the IT department.

External Networking:

- Develops and maintains a network of external partners such as vendors.
- Cultivates relationships with professionals in the broader HR community for professional development and talent identification.

Proficiency Indicators for Advanced HR Professionals:

Leadership Networking:

- Creates opportunities for HR employees to network with higher-level leaders within the organization and in the broader HR community.

- Develops and leverages contacts within and outside the organization, including leaders from other business units, legislative bodies, community leaders, and union heads.

Tips for the SHRM Exam:

- Understand the importance of networking for HR professionals in internal and external contexts.

- Be familiar with strategies for building and maintaining professional relationships.

- Recognize the significance of networking for organizational success and HR leadership.

- Practice identifying opportunities for networking within and outside the organization.

By mastering networking skills and understanding their importance, you'll be better equipped to excel in the Relationship Management aspect of the SHRM CP/SCP exam and your HR career.

Behavioral Competency - Relationship Management

Sub-Competency

(B) Relationship Building

Definition: Networking involves establishing and cultivating professional relationships within and outside the organization, fostering connections that can be leveraged to achieve organizational goals.

Proficiency Indicators for All HR Professionals:

Building Mutual Trust and Respect:

- Develops and maintains mutual trust and respect with colleagues.
- Demonstrates concern for the well-being of colleagues.

Reciprocal Support:

- Establishes a pattern of reciprocal exchanges of support, information, and resources with colleagues.
- Ensures all HR team members and stakeholders feel heard and acknowledged.

Positive Reputation:

- Establishes a solid and positive reputation as an approachable HR professional within and outside the organization.
- Identifies and leverages areas of common interest among stakeholders to foster the success of HR initiatives.

Effective Communication:

- Develops working relationships with supervisors and HR leaders by promptly and effectively responding to work assignments and communicating progress.
- Understands the interests of executives and leaders within the organization.

Utilization of Technology:

- Uses technology to build and maintain strong relationships, especially with individuals who work remotely or at other locations.

Proficiency Indicators for Advanced HR Professionals:

Strategic Relationship Management:

- Develops HR objectives and goals related to relationship management.
- Maintains relationships in the broader HR community through leadership positions in professional organizations.

Continuous Learning and Improvement:

- Leverages relationships to stay informed about best practices and new approaches to building competitive advantage.

Tips for the SHRM Exam:

- Understand the importance of relationship building for HR professionals.
- Familiarize yourself with strategies for fostering trust, respect, and support in professional relationships.
- Recognize the role of effective communication and technology in relationship management.
- Consider the strategic implications of relationship building for HR leadership and organizational success.

By mastering relationship-building skills and understanding their significance, you'll be better prepared for the Relationship Management aspect of the SHRM CP/SCP exam and for success in your HR career.

Behavioral Competency - Relationship Management

Sub-Competency

(C) Teamwork

Definition: Teamwork is a vital sub-competency within the Interpersonal Cluster, essential for fostering collaboration and effective team leadership.

Proficiency Indicators for All HR Professionals:

Building Engaged Relationships:
- Example: Create a team environment where trust is fostered through open communication, offering support with tasks, and involving team members in decision-making.

Fostering Collaboration & Communication:
- Example: Encourage information sharing across departments, actively listen to diverse perspectives within the team, and utilize communication tools that promote open dialogue.

Supporting a Team-Oriented Culture:
- Example: Recognize and reward teamwork achievements, promote team-building activities, and integrate collaboration tools into workflows.

Project Team Participation:
- Example: Actively engage in cross-functional project teams with HR and non-HR colleagues, contributing expertise and fostering collaboration.

Team Leadership:
- Example: When opportunities arise, take the initiative to lead team projects, delegate tasks effectively, and motivate team members to achieve common goals.

Filling Team Gaps:
- Example: Identify areas where the team lacks specific skills or experience, suggest solutions (e.g., training, hiring) to fill these gaps, and ensure team effectiveness.

Proficiency Indicators for Advanced HR Professionals:

Organizational Teamwork Culture:
- Example: Develop and implement HR initiatives that break down departmental silos, promoting collaboration across the organization.

Leading Senior Teams:
- Example: Create and lead high-performing teams, including senior leaders from various departments, leveraging their diverse expertise for strategic decision-making.

HR Initiatives for Teams:
- Example: Design and oversee HR programs that enhance team processes, establish clear communication protocols, and provide training on practical teamwork skills.

Proficiency Level	Indicator	Example
All HR Professionals	Building Engaged Relationships	Create a team environment based on trust, support, and communication
All HR Professionals	Fostering Collaboration & Communication	Encourage information sharing and active listening within the team
All HR Professionals	Supporting a Team-Oriented Culture	Recognize and reward teamwork achievements, promote team-building
All HR Professionals	Project Team Participation	Actively participate in cross-functional project teams
All HR Professionals	Team Leadership	Take initiative to lead team projects, empower team members
All HR Professionals	Filling Team Gaps	Identify skill or experience gaps within the team and suggest solutions
Advanced HR Professionals	Organizational Teamwork Culture	Develop HR initiatives to promote collaboration across departments
Advanced HR Professionals	Leading Senior Teams	Create and lead teams with senior leaders from various departments
Advanced HR Professionals	HR Initiatives for Teams	Design programs to enhance team processes and support teamwork

Behavioral Competency - Relationship Management

Sub-Competency

(D) Negotiation

Definition: Negotiation is a crucial sub-competency for HR professionals, enabling them to reach mutually beneficial agreements with internal and external stakeholders.

Proficiency Indicators for All HR Professionals:

Professional Demeanor:
- Example: Maintain composure, respect, and professionalism throughout the negotiation process, even in challenging situations.

Understanding Needs & Interests:
- Example: Analyze the needs, interests, and bargaining positions of all parties involved to develop a clear picture of negotiation goals.

Concessions for Progress:
- Example: Be prepared to offer strategic concessions that address the other party's concerns without compromising your core interests.

Legal & Regulatory Compliance:
- Example: Ensure all negotiation practices comply with relevant laws and regulations governing negotiation and bargaining in your field.

Evaluation of Progress:
- Example: Regularly assess the progress of negotiations, identifying areas of agreement and potential sticking points.

Identifying Ideal Outcome:
- Example: Define a clear picture of the desired outcome (ideal solution) for the negotiation and adjust strategies based on progress toward that goal. Be prepared to walk away if an agreement is not in your organization's best interest.

Behavioral Competency - Relationship Management

Sub-Competency

(E) Conflict Management

Definition: Conflict Management is a critical sub-competency for HR professionals, equipping them with the skills to resolve disagreements and cultivate a positive work environment effectively.

Proficiency Indicators for All HR Professionals:

Conflict Resolution & Mediation:

- Example: Employ a respectful, impartial approach to resolving conflicts, mediating disagreements between employees, and escalating complex situations when necessary.

Identifying Underlying Causes:

- Example: Focus on uncovering the root cause of conflicts rather than addressing surface-level issues like communication breakdowns or resource scarcity.

Facilitating Difficult Interactions:

- Example: Guide unproductive conversations between employees in a manner that fosters open communication, promotes understanding, and leads to a positive resolution.

Encouraging Productive Conflict:

- Example: Recognize that healthy debate and disagreement can lead to innovation and positive change. Encourage constructive criticism and respectful exchange of ideas within teams.

Positive Role Model:

- Example: Demonstrate effective conflict resolution behaviors in personal interactions, setting a positive example for others.

Counterproductive Conflict Management:

- Example: Identify and proactively address situations where conflict becomes harmful or counterproductive to the workplace environment

Proficiency Indicators for Advanced HR Professionals:

Conflict Resolution Strategies:

- Example: Lead the design and implementation of conflict resolution processes and strategies throughout the organization, including training, mediation programs, or clear escalation protocols.

Senior Leader Facilitation:

- Example: Guide difficult conversations between senior leaders to ensure productive dialogue, address underlying issues, and reach solutions that benefit the organization.

Proactive Conflict Reduction:

- Example: Anticipate potential sources of conflict when proposing new HR initiatives or strategies. Develop proactive measures to mitigate these risks and promote a collaborative environment.

Escalated Conflict Mediation:

- Example: Possess advanced conflict resolution skills to mediate and resolve highly escalated conflicts that lower-level interventions cannot address.

Proficiency Level	Indicator	Example
All HR Professionals	Resolves and/or mediates conflicts respectfully	Uses a fair and impartial approach to mediate conflicts and escalate complex situations when needed
All HR Professionals	Identifies and addresses underlying causes of conflict	Focuses on uncovering the root cause of disagreements rather than just addressing surface-level issues
All HR Professionals	Facilitates difficult interactions among employees	Guides unproductive conversations to promote understanding and reach a positive resolution
All HR Professionals	Encourages productive and respectful task-related conflict	Recognizes the value of healthy debate and disagreement for achieving positive change
All HR Professionals	Serves as a positive role model for productive conflict	Demonstrates productive conflict resolution behaviors to set a positive example for others
All HR Professionals	Identifies and resolves counterproductive or harmful conflict	Proactively addresses situations where conflict becomes destructive to the workplace environment
Advanced HR Professionals	Designs and oversees conflict resolution strategies and processes	Develops and implements conflict resolution programs and guides their use throughout the organization
Advanced HR Professionals	Facilitates difficult interactions among senior leaders	Mediates disputes between senior leaders, ensuring productive dialogue and reaching beneficial solutions
Advanced HR Professionals	Identifies and reduces potential sources of conflict	Anticipates potential conflicts when proposing new HR initiatives and develops plans to mitigate those risks
Advanced HR Professionals	Mediates or resolves escalated conflicts	Possesses advanced skills to mediate highly complex and escalated conflicts that require in-depth intervention

Quiz Corner 4 - RELATIONSHIP MANAGEMENT

Stand-alone Knowledge-Based Questions:

1. Which of the following is NOT a benefit of effective networking for HR professionals?

 a) Increased employee engagement
b) Improved communication and collaboration
c) Enhanced ability to resolve conflict
d) Access to a wider range of qualified job candidates

2) What is a key indicator of a strong working relationship between an HR professional and their supervisor?

a) The HR professional rarely needs to ask for clarification on assignments.
b) The supervisor frequently criticizes the HR professional's work in public.
c) There is open communication and a sense of trust.
d) The HR professional avoids contact with the supervisor whenever possible.

3) When building effective teams, HR professionals should prioritize:

a) Assigning individual tasks with minimal interaction.
b) Establishing clear communication channels and roles.
c) Encouraging competition between team members.
d) Focusing on individual performance metrics.

4) Effective negotiation involves all of the following EXCEPT:

a) Maintaining a professional demeanor
b) Understanding all parties' needs and interests
c) Making emotional appeals
d) Evaluating progress towards an agreement

5) When dealing with interpersonal conflict, an HR professional should prioritize:

a) Taking sides and assigning blame.
b) Identifying the underlying causes of the conflict.
c) Avoiding involvement and letting the employees resolve it themselves.
d) Issuing warnings or disciplinary action.

Quiz Corner 4 - RELATIONSHIP MANAGEMENT

Stand-alone Knowledge-Based Questions:

6) How can HR professionals leverage their network to stay up-to-date on industry trends?

a) Sharing confidential company information with external contacts.
b) Participating in online professional forums and discussions.
c) Focusing solely on building relationships with internal colleagues.
d) Avoiding any professional development activities outside of the organization.

7) What is an effective strategy for developing HR's objectives and goals for relationship management?

a) Focusing solely on building relationships with senior leaders.
b) Establishing clear goals without input from stakeholders.
c) Identifying key areas where strong relationships are crucial for HR initiatives.
d) Delegating relationship management tasks to junior HR staff.

8) How can HR professionals foster an organizational culture that supports collaboration across departments (silo-busting)?

a) Promoting competition and individual performance incentives.
b) Encouraging communication and information sharing across departments.
c) Creating rigid hierarchies and departmental boundaries.
d) Avoiding any cross-departmental projects or initiatives.

9) When negotiating complex HR initiatives, what should HR professionals consider when defining their negotiating boundaries?
a) Focusing solely on the organization's bottom line.
b) Balancing the organization's needs with those of stakeholders.
c) Making concessions without considering potential drawbacks.
d) Negotiating from a position of weakness without clear goals

10) What is the MOST effective strategy for mediating a conflict between senior leaders with different communication styles?

a) Taking sides and assigning blame.
b) Identifying the underlying causes of the conflict.
c) Avoiding involvement and letting the employees resolve it themselves.
d) Issuing warnings or disciplinary action.

Quiz Corner 4 - RELATIONSHIP MANAGEMENT

Scenario-Based Situational Judgment Questions:

1. You are an HR representative attending an industry conference. How can you effectively network with other HR professionals?

a) Stand alone at the refreshment table and avoid conversation.
b) Collect business cards without engaging in meaningful conversations.
c) Identify individuals with shared interests and initiate conversations to build rapport.
d) Focus solely on promoting your own organization's services.

2) A new employee in your department seems very shy and keeps to themselves. How can you help them feel more welcome and build relationships with the team?

a) Assign them individual tasks with minimal interaction with others.
b) Publicly point out their quiet nature and encourage them to be more outgoing.
c) Organize a casual team activity outside of work to encourage interaction.
d) Delegate the task of befriending the new employee to a more outgoing team member.

3) You are working on a project with a team that includes members from different departments who seem hesitant to share their ideas during meetings. What is the best course of action?

a) Publicly call out team members who are not participating.
b) Ignore the issue and hope everyone contributes.
c) Create a safe space for open communication and encourage diverse perspectives.
d) Delegate tasks to each department with minimal collaboration.

4) A disgruntled employee approaches you upset about their compensation package. How should you handle this situation?

a) Dismiss their concerns and tell them there's no room for negotiation.
b) Promise a raise without consulting with management.
c) Schedule a meeting to discuss their concerns and explain the compensation structure.
d) Delegate the task of addressing the employee's concerns to a junior HR staff member.

5) Two employees in your department are having a disagreement about a project deadline. How can you help them resolve the conflict?

a) Take sides and impose a solution without considering their perspectives.
b) Ignore the issue and hope they resolve it themselves.
c) Facilitate a meeting between the employees to discuss their concerns and find common ground.
d) Issue warnings or disciplinary action to both employees.

Quiz Corner 4 - RELATIONSHIP MANAGEMENT

Scenario-Based Situational Judgment Questions:

6) You are an HR manager looking to expand your network of external contacts. What is the MOST effective strategy?

a) Focus solely on building relationships with people within your own company.
b) Participate in industry events and professional organizations.
c) Cold-call potential vendors without any prior research or connection.
d) Avoid any external interactions and focus solely on internal HR initiatives.

7) There seems to be a lack of trust between the HR department and other departments in your organization. How can you begin to rebuild trust?

a) Ignore the issue and hope trust develops over time.
b) Focus on building strong relationships only with HR staff.
c) Schedule meetings with leaders from other departments to understand their concerns and develop solutions.
d) Publicly criticize other departments for their lack of trust in HR.

8) You are tasked with leading a cross-functional team on a complex project. How can you ensure effective teamwork throughout the project?

a) Assign tasks without considering individual strengths or expertise.
b) Clearly define roles, responsibilities, and communication channels.
c) Allow team members to work independently with minimal collaboration.
d) Micromanage the team and dictate every step of the project.

9) You are negotiating a new benefits package with a healthcare vendor. The vendor is proposing a significant price increase. What is the best course of action?

a) Immediately accept the vendor's proposal to avoid further negotiations.
b) Walk away from the negotiation table without considering alternative options.
c) Research alternative vendors and leverage that information to negotiate a better price.
d) Focus solely on the price and ignore other aspects of the proposed benefits package.

10) A cultural misunderstanding is causing conflict between two employees from different backgrounds. How can you effectively address this situation?

a) Assume the employees are being deliberately difficult and issue warnings.
b) Ignore the issue and hope the cultural differences resolve themselves.
c) Educate the employees about cultural differences and promote empathy and understanding.
d) Force the employees to assimilate to the dominant culture in the workplace.

ANSWERS: Quiz Corner 4 - RELATIONSHIP MANAGEMENT

Stand-alone Knowledge-Based Questions:

1. d) Access to a wider range of qualified job candidates
2. c) There is open communication and a sense of trust.
3. b) Establishing clear communication channels and roles.
4. b) Understanding all parties' needs and interests
5. b) Identifying the underlying causes of the conflict.
6. b) Participating in online professional forums and discussions.
7. c) Identifying key areas where strong relationships are crucial for HR initiatives.
8. b) Encouraging communication and information sharing across departments.
9. b) Balancing the organization's needs with those of stakeholders.
10. c) Explaining cultural differences and encouraging empathy and understanding.

Scenario-Based Situational Judgment Questions:

1. c) Identify individuals with shared interests and initiate conversations to build rapport.
2. c) Organize a casual team activity outside of work to encourage interaction.
3. c) Create a safe space for open communication and encourage diverse perspectives.
4. c) Schedule a meeting to discuss their concerns and explain the compensation structure.
5. c) Facilitate a meeting between the employees to discuss their concerns and find common ground.
6. b) Participate in industry events and professional organizations.
7. c) Schedule meetings with leaders from other departments to understand their concerns and develop solutions.
8. b) Clearly define roles, responsibilities, and communication channels.
9. c) Research alternative vendors and leverage that information to negotiate a better price.
10. c) Educate the employees about cultural differences and promote empathy and understanding.

Interpersonal Cluster

Leadership Cluster	Interpersonal Cluster	Business Cluster
Leadership and Navigation	**Relationship Management**	Business Acumen
Ethical Practice	**Communication**	Consultation
Diversity, Equity, and Inclusion	**Global Mindset**	Analytical Aptitude

Communication:

- **Definition:** Knowledge, Skills, Abilities, and Other Qualities required to deliver and understand messages effectively.

- **Examples:** Crafting emails, giving presentations, and actively listening to colleagues.

Sub-competencies:

Sub-competency	Definition	Examples
Delivering Messages	Clearly and concisely conveying information to others.	Planning presentations, tailoring communication style to audience, using visuals effectively.
Exchanging Organizational Information	Sharing and interpreting information across different departments and levels.	Creating reports, translating technical jargon, facilitating communication flow.
Listening	Paying close attention to understand the speaker's message and meaning.	Active listening (focusing on speaker, nodding, asking questions), paraphrasing key points.

Key Concepts:

Elements of Communication:

- Source: Originator of the message.
- Sender: The person who transmits the message.
- Receiver: The person who receives the message.
- Message: The content being communicated.
- Feedback: Response to the message, indicating understanding.

General Communication Techniques:

- Planning communication: Defining goals, audience, and content.
- Active listening: Paying full attention and showing understanding.
- Checking for understanding: Verifying the message is received correctly.
- Asking questions: Clarifying information and encouraging participation.

Communication Techniques for Specialized Situations:

- Giving feedback: Providing constructive criticism for improvement.
- Facilitating meetings: Leading discussions in a productive and focused way.
- Using storytelling: Engaging the audience and conveying messages memorably.
- Creating communication plans: Outlining strategies for message delivery.
- Translating technical jargon: Simplifying complex language for broader understanding.
- Facilitating anonymous communication: Creating safe channels for employee feedback.
- Informal communication: Building relationships through casual interactions.

Communication Media:

- Phone: Verbal communication through telephone.
- Email: Written communication through electronic messages.

- Face-to-face: Direct communication in person.
- Report: Formal document summarizing information.
- Presentation: Formal delivery of information with visuals.
- Social Media: Online platforms for communication and information sharing.
- Town Hall Meetings: Large group meetings for announcements and discussions.
- Videoconference: Virtual meeting using video technology.

Elements of Nonverbal Communication:

- Eye contact: Establishing a connection and showing interest.
- Body language: Posture and facial expressions convey emotions.
- Proximity: Physical distance between communicator and receiver.
- Gestures: Hand and arm movements emphasizing points.

By mastering these concepts and techniques, HR professionals can enhance their communication skills and contribute effectively to organizational success.

Behavioral Competency - Communication

Sub-Competency

(A) Delivering Messages

Definition: Developing and delivering clear, persuasive, and situationally appropriate communications to various audiences.

Importance for HR Professionals: Effective communication is essential for HR professionals to disseminate information, influence decisions, and build trust with stakeholders.

Proficiency Indicators:

Level	Indicator	Example
All HR Professionals	Presents needed information regularly	- Regular HR updates to employees via email or intranet. - Briefing managers on new company policies.
	Refrains from unnecessary information	- Avoiding overloading emails with irrelevant details. - Tailoring presentations to the audience's specific needs.
	Uses audience understanding	- Simplifying technical jargon for a non-technical audience. - Highlighting relevant information for specific stakeholder groups (e.g., benefits for employees).
	Chooses appropriate communication medium	- Using face-to-face meetings for sensitive topics. - Utilizing email for routine updates.
	Uses appropriate business vocabulary	- Maintaining professionalism while avoiding overly complex language. - Tailoring vocabulary to the audience's level of understanding.
	Ensures message clarity and understanding	- Encouraging questions and feedback during presentations. - Verifying understanding by summarizing key points.
	Crafts clear, organized, and error-free messages	- Proofreading written communication carefully. - Structuring presentations with a logical flow.
	Aligns messages with brand	- Using consistent messaging that reflects the organization's values and culture. - Avoiding language that contradicts branding efforts.
	Creates persuasive arguments	- Presenting data and evidence to support recommendations. - Framing messages to resonate with the audience's needs.
Advanced HR Professionals	Fluency in senior leadership language	- Understanding and utilizing terminology relevant to senior management. - Communicating complex financial or strategic concepts effectively.
	Delivers difficult messages effectively	- Presenting negative news with honesty and empathy. - Focusing on solutions and next steps during challenging announcements.
	Presents comfortably to diverse audiences	- Adapting communication style to different cultural backgrounds. - Delivering presentations with confidence and professionalism regardless of audience size.

Tips for Effective Delivery:

- Planning and Preparation: Define your objective, audience, and key message.
- Structure and Organization: Organize content logically with a clear introduction, body, and conclusion.
- Active Voice and Conciseness: Use active voice and concise language to avoid ambiguity.
- Visual Aids: Utilize visuals (e.g., charts, graphs) to support key points and enhance understanding.
- Delivery Style: Speak confidently and with appropriate variation in tone and pace.
- Nonverbal Communication: Maintain good eye contact, positive body language, and an appropriate demeanor.
- Audience Engagement: Encourage questions, address concerns, and actively listen to feedback.

By mastering these proficiency indicators and following effective delivery strategies, HR professionals can enhance communication effectiveness and contribute positively to organizational objectives.

Behavioral Competency - Communication

Sub-Competency

(B) Exchanging Organizational Information Effectively

Definition: Effectively translates and communicates messages among different organizational levels or units.

Importance for HR Professionals: HR acts as a bridge between various departments and leadership. This competency ensures smooth information flow and fosters understanding across the organization.

Proficiency Indicators:

Level	Indicator	Example
All HR Professionals	Communicates HR programs/policies	- Explaining employee benefits to new hires during onboarding. - Providing training sessions on new company policies for all employees.
	Assists non-HR managers	- Guiding managers on conducting performance reviews effectively. - Offering resources and support for handling disciplinary issues.
	Voices support for HR initiatives	- Presenting the rationale behind HR programs to skeptical employees. - Highlighting the positive impact of HR initiatives to external stakeholders (e.g., investors).
	Communicates with HR leaders	- Providing regular updates on HR activities and challenges to senior HR staff. - Seeking guidance and direction from HR leadership on complex issues.
Advanced HR Professionals	Communicates HR vision/strategy	- Presenting HR's strategic goals to senior leadership and explaining their impact on the organization. - Developing communication plans that clearly articulate HR's vision and values to all staff.
	Aligns HR strategy with organizational goals	- Demonstrating how HR initiatives contribute to achieving broader organizational objectives (e.g., increasing employee engagement to boost productivity). - Highlighting the financial benefits of effective HR practices to senior leadership.
	Creates open communication channels	- Implementing internal communication platforms (e.g., intranet, town hall meetings) to facilitate information flow. - Encouraging upward communication by fostering a safe environment for employee feedback.
	Prepares high-visibility messages	- Developing clear and concise communication plans for important HR announcements or organizational changes. - Preparing presentations for board meetings that effectively communicate crucial HR information to senior leaders.

Strategies for Effective Information Exchange:

- Understanding Audience Needs: Tailor communication to address the specific information needs of each audience.

- Clarity and Concision: Use concise language and avoid technical jargon whenever possible.

- Multiple Communication Channels: Utilize various communication channels (e.g., email, face-to-face meetings, intranet) to reach diverse audiences.

- Active Listening: Actively listen to concerns and questions to ensure clarity and understanding.

- Feedback Mechanisms: Establish precise feedback mechanisms to encourage two-way communication.

- Transparency and Openness: Communicate information transparently and openly, fostering trust and credibility.

Behavioral Competency - Communication

Sub-Competency

(C) Listening

Definition: Effectively translates and communicates messages among different organizational levels or units.

Importance for HR Professionals: HR acts as a bridge between various departments and leadership. This competency ensures smooth information flow and fosters understanding across the organization.

Level	Indicator	Example
All HR Professionals	Actively listens	- Maintaining eye contact and showing attentiveness while employees are speaking. - Paraphrasing and summarizing key points to ensure understanding.
	Empathy during listening	- Acknowledging and validating employee emotions during difficult conversations. - Considering an employee's perspective when addressing their concerns.

Level	Indicator	Example
	Openness to different viewpoints	- Encouraging employees to express opposing ideas or concerns without judgment. - Seeking diverse perspectives when making decisions.
	Seeks clarification	- Asking clarifying questions to understand ambiguous information. - Repeating back instructions or requests to confirm understanding.
	Timely responses	- Promptly responding to employee inquiries or messages. - Communicating resolutions or updates on issues raised by stakeholders.
	Interprets context	- Considering the underlying reasons behind employee communication. - Understanding the emotional context of a situation.
	Solicits feedback	- Conducting regular employee surveys to gauge satisfaction and identify areas for improvement. - Encouraging managers to actively seek feedback from their teams.
Advanced HR Professionals	Promotes upward communication	- Organizing "open door" policies where employees can feel comfortable sharing feedback with leadership. - Implementing anonymous feedback channels (e.g., suggestion boxes) to encourage communication.
	Gathers organization-wide feedback	- Conducting HR-specific surveys to gather feedback on HR programs and initiatives. - Organizing focus groups to understand employee experiences with HR functions.

Tips for Effective Listening:

Focus on the Speaker: Give the speaker your full attention and minimize distractions.

Nonverbal Cues: Maintain eye contact and positive body language (e.g., nodding)**.**

Active Listening Techniques: Paraphrase critical points and ask clarifying questions.

Show Empathy: Acknowledge and validate the speaker's emotions.

Avoid Interruptions: Allow the speaker to finish their thoughts before responding.

Defer Judgment: Listen objectively without formulating judgments prematurely.

Quiz Corner 5 - Communication

Stand-alone Knowledge-Based Questions:

1. Which of the following is NOT an element of communication?

A) Source
B) Sender
C) Receiver
D) Feedback

2) Which communication technique involves simplifying complex language for a broader audience?

A) Active listening
B) Checking for understanding
C) Translating technical jargon
D) Delivering presentations

3) Which communication medium is best suited for delivering a complex presentation with visuals?

A) Phone call
B) Email
C) Face-to-face meeting
D) Presentation

4) Nonverbal communication includes all of the following EXCEPT:

A) Eye contact
B) Body language
C) Tone of voice
D) Proximity

5) Effective listening involves all of the following EXCEPT:

A) Maintaining eye contact
B) Showing empathy
C) Interrupting the speaker
D) Asking clarifying questions

Quiz Corner 5 - Communication

Scenario-Based Situational Judgment Questions:

1. You are tasked with presenting a new company policy on remote work to a diverse group of employees with varying levels of technical expertise. How would you ensure clear communication and understanding for everyone?

A) Deliver a technical presentation using industry jargon.
B) Briefly summarize the policy in a company-wide email.
C) Tailor your explanation to the audience's technical background, using visuals and providing examples.
D) Ask employees to research the policy details beforehand individually.

2) A disgruntled employee approaches you upset about a negative performance review. During the conversation, they become emotional and raise their voice. How do you respond most effectively?

A) Dismiss their concerns and tell them to focus on improvement.
B) Interrupt them and explain the performance review process.
C) Actively listen, acknowledge their emotions, and offer to discuss the feedback in more detail later.
D) Ask them to submit their concerns in writing for formal review.

3) You are the HR manager for a company with multiple departments experiencing communication silos. What steps can you take to improve information flow across the organization?

- A) Ignore the issue and hope communication improves on its own.
- B) Focus solely on improving communication within the HR department.
- C) Facilitate cross-departmental meetings and workshops to encourage collaboration and knowledge sharing.
- D) Issue a company-wide memo emphasizing the importance of communication.

4) You are tasked with delivering difficult news about a company restructuring to senior management. How can you ensure the message is delivered effectively and respectfully?

A) Briefly announce the news in an email without offering explanations.
B) Focus solely on the negative aspects of the restructuring.
C) Prepare a clear and concise presentation outlining the reasons for the restructuring, potential impact, and support for affected employees. (Correct)
D) Schedule one-on-one meetings to deliver the news to each senior manager individually.

5) Your company is implementing a new employee feedback survey. How can you encourage employees to participate honestly and openly?

- A) Make the survey mandatory and threaten disciplinary action for non-participation.
- B) Share only positive feedback results with senior management.
- C) Guarantee anonymity and emphasize the importance of honest feedback for improving the work environment.
- D) Offer rewards to employees who complete the survey with positive feedback.

ANSWERS: Quiz Corner 5 - Communication

Stand-alone Knowledge-Based Questions:

1. A) Source
2. C) Translating technical jargon
3. C) Face-to-face meeting
4. C) Tone of voice
5. C) Interrupting the speaker

Scenario-Based Situational Judgment Questions:

1. C) Tailor your explanation to the audience's technical background, using visuals and providing examples.
2. C) Actively listen, acknowledge their emotions, and offer to discuss the feedback in more detail later.
3. C) Facilitate cross-departmental meetings and workshops to encourage collaboration and knowledge sharing.
4. C) Prepare a clear and concise presentation outlining the reasons for the restructuring, potential impact, and support for affected employees.
5. C) Guarantee anonymity and emphasize the importance of honest feedback for improving the work environment.

Interpersonal Cluster

Leadership Cluster	Interpersonal Cluster	Business Cluster
Leadership and Navigation	**Relationship Management**	Business Acumen
Ethical Practice	**Communication**	Consultation
Diversity, Equity, and Inclusion	**Global Mindset**	Analytical Aptitude

Global Mindset :

- Global Mindset is a crucial competency for HR professionals in today's interconnected world. It encompasses the knowledge, skills, and abilities required to value diversity, interact effectively across cultures, and promote inclusivity in the workplace.

Sub-competencies:

Sub-competency	Description
Operating in a Culturally Diverse Workplace	Understanding cultural norms, values, and communication styles; mitigating unconscious bias; fostering collaboration across cultures.
Operating in a Global Environment	Adapting HR practices to international regulations; managing geographically dispersed teams; understanding global business practices.
Advocating for a Culturally Diverse and Inclusive Workplace	Promoting diversity initiatives; creating a welcoming environment; encouraging open communication and valuing diverse perspectives.

Key Concepts:

Cultural Norms, Values, and Dimensions:

- Understanding frameworks like Hofstede's Six Dimensions (e.g., power distance, individualism).
- Models include Hall's (high-context vs. low-context communication) and Trompenaars' (relationships vs. rules).

Bridging and Leveraging Differences:

- Techniques like Employee Resource Groups (ERGs), Reverse Mentorship, Sensitivity Training, and Focus Groups.

Best Practices for Global Workforces:

- Translation of policies and communication materials.
- Consideration of time zone differences in scheduling.
- Awareness of legal and cultural variations in business practices.

Examples:

- **Scenario:** A US company expands to China. HR adapts the recruitment process based on Chinese cultural values, incorporating group exercises and panel interviews.

- **Scenario:** A multinational company, considering cultural differences, implements a global performance management system. They emphasize face-to-face feedback sessions tailored to employees' cultural backgrounds.

Remember:

Developing a global mindset is ongoing. Actively seeking knowledge, embracing diverse perspectives, and implementing inclusive practices are key to creating a thriving global work environment.

Behavioral Competency - Global Mindset

Sub-Competency

(A) Operating in a Culturally Diverse Workplace

This sub-competency emphasizes openness and respect when working with colleagues from diverse cultural backgrounds. HR professionals play a critical role in fostering a positive and inclusive work environment that celebrates these differences

Proficiency Indicators:.

Level	Indicator	Example
All HR Professionals	General Awareness & Understanding	- Attends workshops on cultural competency. - Reads articles or books on specific cultural norms.
	Adapts Behavior	- Uses more formal language when communicating with colleagues from cultures valuing hierarchical structures (e.g., Japan). - Avoids humor that may not translate well across cultures.
	Acceptance of Colleagues	- Organizes team-building activities that encourage interaction between diverse employees. - Recognizes and celebrates cultural holidays and traditions.
	Promotes Benefits of Diversity	- Includes diversity statistics in presentations highlighting the value of a diverse workforce (e.g., increased innovation). - Shares success stories showcasing how diverse teams achieved goals.
	Promotes Inclusion	- Creates opportunities for participation in meetings and decision-making for all employees, regardless of background. - Reviews company policies and procedures to ensure they are unbiased and inclusive.
	Conducts Cross-cultural Business	- Researches cultural norms and business practices before international business trips. - Adjusts communication style (e.g., direct vs. indirect) based on the business partner's cultural background.
Advanced HR Professionals	Drives Culture of Diversity & Inclusion	- Develops and implements comprehensive diversity and inclusion initiatives (e.g., unconscious bias training, ERGs). - Creates a safe space for open communication and feedback about cultural differences.
	Strategic Connection: Diversity & Success	- Presents data on how diversity fosters innovation, creativity, and problem-solving in the workplace. - Demonstrates how inclusive practices contribute to improved employee engagement and organizational performance.

Understanding Cultural Differences:

Cultural Frameworks:

These frameworks offer a lens to understand cultural variations in communication styles, decision-making processes, and work approaches. Some popular models include:

Framework	Dimension	Example
Hofstede's Six Dimensions	Power Distance (High vs. Low)	- High Power Distance: Employees expect clear hierarchies and may be less comfortable directly questioning superiors (e.g., Mexico). - Low Power Distance: Employees value collaboration and may be more comfortable offering different viewpoints (e.g., Denmark).
	Individualism vs. Collectivism	- Individualistic Cultures: Focus on personal achievement and independence (e.g., United States). - Collectivistic Cultures: Emphasize group harmony and prioritize the needs of the collective (e.g., China).
	Masculinity vs. Femininity	- Masculine Cultures: Value assertiveness, competition, and material success (e.g., Japan). - Feminine Cultures: Emphasize cooperation, relationship building, and quality of life (e.g., Sweden).
	Uncertainty Avoidance (High vs. Low)	- High Uncertainty Avoidance: Prefer clear rules, structure, and dislike ambiguity (e.g., Germany). - Low Uncertainty Avoidance: More comfortable with flexibility and adapting to change (e.g., Greece).
	Long-Term Orientation vs. Short-Term Orientation	- Long-Term Orientation: Value perseverance, saving, and future planning (e.g., China). - Short-Term Orientation: Focus on the present, immediate gratification, and respect for tradition (e.g., Venezuela).
	Indulgence vs. Restraint	- Indulgent Cultures: Value leisure time, enjoying life, and having fun (e.g., Brazil). - Restrained Cultures: Emphasize self-control, frugality, and work ethic (e.g., South Korea).

Remember: These frameworks are generalizations and individual experiences may vary. Cultural frameworks are most helpful as a starting point to understand potential differences and avoid stereotypical assumptions.

Cultural Framework	Definition	Example
Hall's Communication Styles	Hall's theory distinguishes between high-context and low-context communication cultures. In high-context cultures, much of the information is implied and understood through context, whereas in low-context cultures, communication is more direct and explicit.	Example: In high-context cultures like Japan, much of the meaning is conveyed through nonverbal cues and implicit messages. In contrast, in low-context cultures like Germany, communication tends to be more direct and explicit, with less reliance on context.
Schein's Organizational Culture Assumptions	Schein's model explores the underlying assumptions and beliefs that shape organizational culture. It identifies three levels: artifacts (visible elements), espoused values (stated beliefs and values), and underlying assumptions (unconscious beliefs and perceptions).	Example: In an organization where employees are encouraged to speak up and challenge authority (espoused value), the underlying assumption may be that innovation and creativity are valued, leading to a culture of openness and collaboration.
Trompenaars' Dimensions	Trompenaars identifies cultural dimensions such as relationships vs. rules (how individuals balance personal relationships with adherence to rules) and specificity vs. diffuseness (how individuals communicate with specificity or ambiguity).	Example: In cultures that prioritize relationships, such as many Asian cultures, decisions may be influenced by personal connections rather than strictly following rules or procedures. In contrast, in cultures that value rules, such as many Western cultures, decisions are often based on adherence to established rules and regulations. Specificity vs. diffuseness refers to how directly or indirectly people communicate. In specific cultures like Germany, communication tends to be precise and explicit, whereas in diffuse cultures like Arab countries, communication may be more indirect and open to interpretation.

Strategies for Building a Culturally Diverse Workplace:

- **Employee Resource Groups (ERGs)**
- **Reverse Mentorship**
- **Sensitivity Training**
- **Intercultural Communication Training**
- **Celebration of Diversity**

Creating a work environment where everyone feels valued and respected is key to harnessing the benefits of cultural diversity.

Behavioral Competency - Global Mindset

Sub-Competency
(B) Operating in a Global Environment

In today's interconnected world, HR professionals must be adept at managing the complexities of a global workplace. This sub-competency focuses on effectively navigating these challenges to achieve organizational goals.

Proficiency Indicators:

Level	Indicator	Example
All HR Professionals	Global Business Understanding	* Researches the global market landscape for the company's industry. * Analyzes how global trends impact the organization's operations.
	Tailoring HR Initiatives	* Adapts recruitment strategies to attract qualified candidates from different countries. * Develops training programs that consider cultural sensitivities.
	Compliance with Global Regulations	* Ensures HR policies and procedures comply with local labor laws and regulations (e.g., minimum wage, paid leave). * Stays updated on international employment regulations.
	Global HR Trends	* Incorporates best practices from global HR trends into company policies (e.g., remote work options). * Analyzes how global talent shortages impact workforce planning.
	Global Mindset & Local Sensitivity	* Values diverse perspectives and experiences from a global workforce. * Recognizes the importance of adapting HR practices to local needs.
	Managing Contradictions	* Identifies potential conflicts between company policies and local cultural norms. * Develops solutions that respect both global and local practices (e.g., flexible dress code policies).
Advanced HR Professionals	Global HR Strategy	* Aligns HR strategy with the organization's global goals and competencies (e.g., developing intercultural communication skills for a multinational workforce). * Promotes a global talent management strategy to attract and retain top talent worldwide.
	Strategic Use of Global HR Knowledge	* Leverages expertise on global HR trends to identify new opportunities (e.g., expanding into emerging markets). * Analyzes how economic conditions in different countries affect recruitment and compensation strategies.
	Diversity & Inclusion in Global Strategy	* Integrates diversity and inclusion considerations into the global HR strategy. * Ensures global HR programs promote an inclusive work environment for employees from diverse backgrounds.

Challenges of Operating in a Global Environment:

- **Cultural Differences**: Communication styles, work ethic, and decision-making processes vary significantly across cultures.

- **Labor Laws and Regulations**: HR professionals must comply with a complex web of country-specific employment laws.

- **Global Talent Management**: Attracting, developing, and retaining talent in a competitive global market.

- **Economic and Political Conditions**: Economic fluctuations and political instability can impact workforce planning and compensation strategies.

Strategies for Success:

- **Developing a Global Mindset**: HR professionals need to be open to new perspectives and understand the impact of cultural differences.

- **Staying Informed:** Regularly update knowledge on global HR trends, economic conditions, and legal developments in different countries.

- **Building Relationships**: Establish strong relationships with HR professionals in other countries to share best practices and address challenges collaboratively.

- **Leveraging Technology**: Utilize technology to facilitate communication, collaboration, and talent management across borders (e.g., video conferencing, cloud-based HR platforms).

Remember:

Operating in a global environment requires flexibility, adaptability, and a commitment to continuous learning. By understanding the complexities of the global workplace, HR professionals can develop effective strategies to achieve organizational success.

Behavioral Competency - Global Mindset

Sub-Competency

(C) Advocating for a Culturally Diverse and Inclusive Workplace

HR professionals are critical in fostering a workplace that values diversity and inclusion. This sub-competency focuses on designing, implementing, and promoting practices that ensure everyone feels respected, valued, and empowered to contribute their best.

Proficiency Indicators:

Level	Indicator	Example
All HR Professionals	Culture of Diversity & Inclusion	* Participate in diversity and inclusion initiatives (e.g., ERGs, unconscious bias training). * Promote the benefits of diversity and inclusion through internal communication channels (e.g., company newsletter, employee intranet).
	Aligning Policies & Practices	* Review company policies and procedures to identify and address potential biases (e.g., recruitment processes, performance evaluations). * Recommend changes to policies that promote equal opportunities for all employees.
	Designing Inclusive Programs	* Develop or implement HR programs that attract diverse candidates (e.g., targeted job postings on diverse platforms, diverse interview panels). * Create training programs focused on cultural sensitivity and understanding (e.g., workshops on communication styles across cultures).
	Consistent & Respectful Application	* Ensure fair and consistent application of HR policies and procedures for all employees. * Address any incidents of discrimination or bias promptly and effectively according to established policies.
Advanced HR Professionals	Evaluating Workplace Culture	* Conduct surveys or focus groups to assess employee perceptions of the company's culture regarding diversity and inclusion. * Analyze data to identify areas where the organization can improve inclusivity.
	Developing HR Initiatives	* Design and implement comprehensive diversity and inclusion programs tailored to the organization's needs (e.g., mentoring programs for diverse employees, unconscious bias training for leadership at all levels). * Advocate for budget allocation to support these initiatives.
	Learning & Development Programs	* Collaborate with training and development specialists to create engaging learning opportunities on diversity and cultural sensitivity for all employee levels (e.g., interactive workshops, online modules with accessibility features). * Ensure training programs cater to diverse learning styles (e.g., visual, auditory, kinesthetic).
	Driving HR Strategy	* Integrate diversity and inclusion goals into the overall HR strategy. * Track and measure the impact of diversity and inclusion initiatives on key metrics (e.g., employee engagement, retention, workforce demographics).
	Celebrating Diversity	* Organize events that celebrate cultural diversity (e.g., international food festivals, cultural heritage presentations). * Recognize and reward employees who champion diversity and inclusion through awards or nominations.

Importance of Diversity and Inclusion:

Benefit	Description	Example
Improved Innovation & Creativity	Diverse teams bring together different perspectives and experiences, leading to more creative solutions.	A multicultural marketing team develops a campaign that resonates with a wider audience due to their varied cultural understanding.
Enhanced Problem-Solving	A variety of viewpoints allows for a more comprehensive approach to problem-solving.	An engineering team composed of individuals with different backgrounds tackles a technical challenge from multiple angles, leading to an effective solution.
Stronger Employer Brand	Companies with a reputation for diversity and inclusion attract top talent from a wider pool of candidates.	A company recognized for its inclusive work environment receives a surge of applications from qualified candidates seeking a welcoming and supportive workplace.
Increased Employee Engagement & Retention	Employees feel valued and respected in an inclusive work environment, leading to higher engagement and lower turnover.	A company with a strong focus on diversity and inclusion experiences a significant decrease in employee turnover compared to industry averages.

Challenges of Creating a Diverse and Inclusive Workplace:

- **Unconscious Bias**: Everyone has biases, but HR professionals can help employees recognize and mitigate them through training.

- **Communication Barriers:** Cultural differences can lead to misunderstandings. Training on intercultural communication can help bridge these gaps.

- **Lack of Representation:** Certain groups may be underrepresented in the workforce. HR can develop strategies to attract and retain diverse talent (e.g., targeted recruitment efforts and partnering with diversity-focused organizations).

Strategies for Building a Diverse and Inclusive Workplace:
- Diversity & Inclusion Task Force: Establish a dedicated team to develop and implement diversity and inclusion initiatives.
- Employee Resource Groups (ERGs): Provide support networks and a sense of belonging for employees from similar backgrounds.
- Mentorship Programs: Connect experienced employees with diverse mentees to support career growth and development.
- Accountability Measures: Set clear goals and track progress on diversity and inclusion metrics (e.g., workforce demographics, employee engagement surveys).
- Regular Communication: Communicate the organization's commitment to diversity and inclusion through various channels (e.g., company-wide meetings, newsletters).

Building a Diverse and Inclusive Workplace - Additional Tips:

Inclusive Recruitment Practices:
- Utilize diverse job boards and professional organizations to reach a wider talent pool.
- Standardize interview processes and use diverse interview panels to minimize bias.
- Develop clear and objective job descriptions that focus on skills and qualifications.

Focus on Accessibility:
- Ensure career websites and application materials are accessible to individuals with disabilities.
- Provide reasonable accommodations during the interview process and for employees with disabilities.

Inclusive Work Environment:

- Offer flexible work arrangements to accommodate diverse needs and lifestyles.
- Organize team-building activities that celebrate cultural differences.
- Recognize and reward employees who demonstrate inclusive behaviors.

Leadership Commitment:

- Senior leadership must be visibly committed to diversity and inclusion for these initiatives to be successful.
- Leaders should hold themselves and others accountable for fostering an inclusive work environment.

Quiz Corner 6 - GLOBAL MINDSET

Stand-alone Knowledge-Based Questions:

1. According to Hofstede's framework, which dimension focuses on the discomfort people feel with ambiguity? (Select the BEST answer)

a. Power Distance
b. Individualism vs. Collectivism
c. Uncertainty Avoidance
d. Long-Term Orientation vs. Short-Term Orientation

2) Which of the following is an example of a workplace technique for bridging cultural differences? (Select the BEST answer)

a. Implementing a global performance management system without considering cultural variations in communication styles.
b. Establishing Employee Resource Groups (ERGs) for employees from similar backgrounds.
c. Only promoting employees from the dominant culture in the organization.
d. Failing to adapt communication styles to different cultural audiences.

3) A company with a global workforce is developing a new anti-discrimination policy. Which of the following is the most significant consideration for the HR department?

a. Only translate the policy into the most common languages spoken by employees.
b. Ensuring the policy complies with all operating countries' local labor laws and regulations.
c. Using legal jargon that may be difficult for some employees to understand.
d. Focusing solely on the company's headquarters country's legal requirements.

4) What is the benefit of a diverse and inclusive workplace?

a. Increased risk of misunderstandings due to cultural differences.
b. Lower employee engagement and morale.
c. Reduced innovation and creativity.
d. Enhanced problem-solving and decision-making due to a variety of perspectives.

5) Which of the following is NOT a proficiency indicator for all HR professionals related to operating in a culturally diverse workplace?

a. Demonstrates a general awareness and understanding of cultural differences.
b. Develop and implements comprehensive diversity and inclusion programs
c. Adapts behavior to navigate different cultural situations.
d. Promotes the benefits of a diverse and inclusive workforce.

Quiz Corner 6 - GLOBAL MINDSET

Stand-alone Knowledge-Based Questions:

6. Trompenaars' framework includes a dimension that focuses on how people view relationships with others. What is this dimension called?

a. Universalism vs. Particularism
b. Individualism vs. Collectivism
c. Power Distance
d. Achievement vs. Ascription

7. When working with a team from a high uncertainty avoidance culture, which communication styles would be MOST effective?

a. Direct and concise communication with limited elaboration. (CORRECT)
b. Indirect communication with a focus on building relationships before getting down to business.
c. Highly detailed and technical communication using jargon.
d. Open-ended questions and brainstorming sessions that encourage a variety of perspectives.

8. A company with a presence in multiple countries is developing a new employee onboarding program. Which factors should the HR department consider to ensure the program is effective across cultures?

a. Standardizing the onboarding process for all locations to ensure consistency.
b. Tailoring the program content to address cultural norms and communication styles in different countries.
c. Focusing solely on company policies and procedures without providing context or cultural explanations.
d. Delivering the program entirely online without any in-person interaction.

9. What is a potential challenge of managing a global workforce?

a. Increased opportunities for innovation due to diverse perspectives.
b. Streamlined communication processes due to standardized practices.
c. Potential for misunderstandings due to cultural differences.
d. Reduced administrative burden for HR professionals.

10) According to Geert Hofstede, which cultural dimension focuses on the degree to which a society encourages thrift and saving for the future?

a. Power Distance
b. Individualism vs. Collectivism
c. Uncertainty Avoidance
d. Long-Term Orientation vs. Short-Term Orientation

Quiz Corner 6 - Global Mindset

Scenario-Based Situational Judgment Questions:

Scenario 1:

You are an HR representative for a US-based tech company expanding its operations to China. During your first meeting with the new Chinese team, you notice they are hesitant to speak up and offer their ideas during the brainstorming session.

Question:

Which of the following actions would be MOST appropriate in this situation?

(A) Call on specific team members by name to share their ideas.
(B) Ask open-ended questions and encourage everyone to participate.
(C) Briefly explain your expectations for active participation.
(D) Move on to the next agenda item if no one volunteers their ideas.

Scenario 2:

You are the HR manager for a global marketing agency. The agency is developing a new advertising campaign for a client's product launch. The campaign will be targeted towards a European audience, but the team mainly consists of employees from the United States and Asia.

Question:

What is the BEST course of action for the HR manager to ensure the campaign is culturally appropriate for the European market?

(A) Assign the project solely to the employees from the United States.
(B) Assemble a diverse team with representatives from different regions and research European cultural norms.
(C) Rely solely on the client's input for cultural considerations.
(D) Ask the employees from Asia to handle the non-visual aspects of the campaign.

Scenario 3:
You are the HR Business Partner for a manufacturing company that is opening a new factory in Mexico. The company culture at headquarters is very informal and casual. However, you've learned that Mexican culture tends to be more formal and hierarchical.

Question:

How can you best approach this cultural difference to ensure a smooth integration of the new Mexican employees into the company culture?

(A) Explain to the Mexican employees that they must adapt to the company's informal culture.
(B) Develop a communication plan that acknowledges cultural differences and outlines strategies for respectful and effective interactions between headquarters and the Mexican factory.
(C) Advise the headquarters team to maintain their informal style and avoid making changes.
(D) Focus solely on training the Mexican employees on company policies and procedures.

Quiz Corner 6 - Global Mindset

Scenario-Based Situational Judgment Questions:

Scenario 4:

You are the HR Director for a multinational financial services company. A German employee has filed a complaint alleging that they were discriminated against during a promotion process. The employee feels their American manager overlooked them in favor of a US colleague.

Question:

What steps should you take as the HR Director to investigate this complaint effectively?

(A) Ask the American manager to explain their decision and assume their explanation is accurate.
(B) Conduct a thorough investigation that includes interviewing the German employee, the American manager, and any other relevant witnesses. Consider cultural differences that may be impacting perceptions.
(C) Dismiss the complaint without investigation due to the lack of concrete evidence.
(D) Focus solely on the American manager's perspective to determine if they violated company policy.

Scenario 5

You are the HR Manager for a large retail company with headquarters in the United States and a branch office in France. The company plans to implement a new performance management system that utilizes a more direct and critical feedback approach. However, you've received concerns from some French employees who feel this method might be too harsh and could damage team morale.

Question:

How should you approach this situation to ensure a successful rollout of the new performance management system while addressing the concerns of the French employees?

Here are some options to consider:

(A) Forcefully implement the new system, explaining that it is the company standard, and there is no room for negotiation.
(B) Completely scrap the new system and develop one tailored to the French culture.
(C) Develop a modified training program for the French employees that explains the rationale behind the new system and provides guidance on delivering constructive feedback in a culturally sensitive manner.
(D) Delay the implementation of the system indefinitely to avoid any potential cultural clashes.

ANSWERS: Quiz Corner 6 - Global Mindset

Stand-alone Knowledge-Based Questions:

1. c. Uncertainty Avoidance (CORRECT)
2. b. Establishing Employee Resource Groups (ERGs) for employees from similar backgrounds. (CORRECT)
3. b. Ensuring the policy complies with all operating countries' local labor laws and regulations. (CORRECT)
4. d. Enhanced problem-solving and decision-making due to a variety of perspectives. (CORRECT)
5. b. Develops and implements comprehensive diversity and inclusion programs
6. c. Power Distance (This dimension focuses on hierarchy and power structures.)
7. a. Direct and concise communication with limited elaboration. (CORRECT)
8. b. Tailoring the program content to address cultural norms and communication styles in different countries. (CORRECT)
9. c. Potential for misunderstandings due to cultural differences. (CORRECT)
10. d. Long-Term Orientation vs. Short-Term Orientation (CORRECT)

Scenario-Based Situational Judgment Questions:

1. (B) Ask open-ended questions and encourage everyone to participate. (CORRECT - This approach is more inclusive and culturally sensitive, allowing the team to feel comfortable contributing.)
2. (B) Assemble a diverse team with representatives from different regions and research European cultural norms. (CORRECT - This approach leverages the team's diverse perspectives and ensures cultural sensitivity.)
3. (B) Develop a communication plan that acknowledges cultural differences and outlines strategies for respectful and effective interactions between headquarters and the Mexican factory. (CORRECT - This approach recognizes the difference and seeks a solution that respects both cultures.)
4. (B) Conduct a thorough investigation that includes interviewing the German employee, the American manager, and other relevant witnesses. Consider cultural differences that may be impacting perceptions. (CORRECT - A thorough investigation and cultural sensitivity are essential.)
5. (C) Develop a modified training program for the French employees that explains the rationale behind the new system and provides guidance on delivering constructive feedback in a culturally sensitive manner. (CORRECT - This option addresses the concerns and equips employees with the skills to adapt.)

5. Behavioral Competencies- Business Cluster

Business Cluster

Leadership Cluster	Interpersonal Cluster	Business Cluster
Leadership and Navigation	Relationship Management	*Business Acumen*
Ethical Practice	Communication	*Consultation*
Diversity, Equity, and Inclusion	Global Mindset	*Analytical Aptitude*

This cluster focuses on the HR professional's ability to understand and contribute to the organization's business side. It encompasses three key behavioral competencies:

Business Acumen: This competency highlights the HR professional's ability to see the "big picture" of the business and understand how HR initiatives impact organizational goals.

Consultation: Effective HR professionals are trusted advisors to business leaders, providing strategic guidance and solutions on people-related issues.

Analytical Aptitude: The ability to gather, analyze, and interpret data is crucial for making informed HR decisions aligned with business needs.

Key Responsibilities:

Strategic Alignment:
- Ensure HR activities contribute to the organization's overall strategy.

Business Understanding:
- Deep comprehension of the industry, competitors, and business model.

HR Solutions Design & Implementation:
- Developing and implementing HR programs addressing specific business needs (e.g., talent acquisition strategies for growth initiatives).

Change Management:
- Championing and leading change initiatives impacting HR practices and policies.

Data-Driven Decision Making:
- Utilizing data analytics to inform HR strategies and measure the impact of HR programs on business outcomes (e.g., cost savings, employee engagement).

Competency	Example Activities
Business Acumen	- Translate business needs into actionable HR strategies. - Contribute to financial planning processes by understanding HR costs.
Consultation	- Collaborate with business leaders to identify human capital challenges. - Provide recommendations on talent management strategies to improve workforce performance.
Analytical Aptitude	- Analyze workforce demographics to identify potential skills gaps. - Track HR metrics (e.g., turnover rate, time to hire) to measure program effectiveness.

Remember: HR professionals play a vital role in driving business success. A strong understanding of the business and its needs is critical for developing and implementing effective HR strategies.

Behavioral Competency - (1) Business Acumen

Understanding the organization's business operations and translating that knowledge into effective HR strategies.

Key Components:

Business & Competitive Awareness:

- Comprehending key business terms and concepts (e.g., competitive advantage, profit and loss, KPIs).
- Analyzing business documents (e.g., strategic plans, contracts) to understand business goals and challenges.

Business Analysis:

- Gathering and analyzing data using business intelligence tools and techniques (e.g., trend analysis, balanced scorecard).
- Understanding financial statements (e.g., balance sheet, P&L) to assess the organization's financial health.

Strategic Alignment:

- Developing HR initiatives that align with the organization's overall strategic direction.
- Building a solid business case for HR programs, demonstrating their benefits and ROI.

Importance:

- Strong business acumen allows HR professionals to:
- Design HR programs that address real business needs.
- Partner effectively with business leaders.
- Demonstrate the value of HR to the organization.
- By developing business acumen, HR professionals can become strategic business partners, driving organizational success.

Behavioral Competency - Business Acumen

Table: Business Acumen - Key Concepts & Examples

Concept	Description	Example
Competitive Advantage	What sets your organization apart from competitors?	Unique product offering, superior customer service.
Profit & Loss (P&L)	Summarizes revenues and expenses over a specific period.	Helps assess profitability.
Revenue	Total income generated from sales of goods or services.	Used to evaluate sales performance.
Key Performance Indicators (KPIs)	Metrics that track progress towards strategic goals.	Employee engagement score, customer satisfaction rating.
Business Plan	Outlines the organization's business model and future plans.	Guides resource allocation and strategic direction.
SWOT Analysis	Evaluates Strengths, Weaknesses, Opportunities, and Threats.	Provides insights for strategic decision-making.
Return on Investment (ROI)	Measures the financial benefit of an investment.	Helps evaluate the effectiveness of HR programs.

Behavioral Competency - Business Acumen

Sub-Competency

(A) Business and Competitive Awareness

- **Definition:** Grasping internal and external factors impacting the organization.

Key Responsibilities

Internal Knowledge is understanding the organization's:
- Operations and functions
- Products and services

External Awareness is to stay informed about the broader environment through **PESTLE** analysis:

- **P**olitical
- **E**conomic
- **S**ocial
- **T**echnological
- **L**egal
- **E**nvironmental

Proficiency Indicators:

All HR Professionals:

- Utilize internal and external resources to learn about the organization's business.
- Apply knowledge of the business and PESTLE trends to inform HR decisions and program design.

Advanced HR Professionals:

- Leverage business intelligence from PESTLE trends to shape HR strategy and long-term goals.
- Utilize expertise in the organization's business when setting HR's strategic direction.
- Understand the labor market dynamics to manage and attract talent effectively.
- Advocate for HR strategies and goals by engaging with government policies and regulations.

Factor	Description	Example
Internal	Operations & Functions	Understanding the production process, distribution channels, or customer service procedures.
	Products & Services	Knowing the features and benefits of the company's offerings.

Factor	Description	Example
External	Political	Government policies affecting labor laws.
	Economic	Economic recession leading to hiring freezes.
	Social	Shifting demographics influencing diversity initiatives.
	Technological	Automation requiring upskilling or reskilling programs.
	Legal	Changes in labor laws impacting employee benefits.
	Environmental	Sustainability initiatives affecting recruitment strategies.

Importance:

Business and competitive awareness allows HR professionals to:

- Design HR programs that address real business needs and respond to external changes.
- Partner effectively with business leaders by understanding the broader context.
- Demonstrate the strategic value of HR by aligning initiatives with the organization's goals.

By staying informed and applying knowledge of the business environment, HR professionals can play a proactive role in driving organizational success.

Behavioral Competency - Business Acumen

Sub-Competency

(B) Business Analysis

- **Definition:** Utilize business analysis tools to inform HR strategies.

Key Responsibilities:

HR & Business Metrics:
- Conduct a cost-benefit analysis of HR programs.
- Evaluate HR program effectiveness using KPIs.
- Example: Analyze cost per hire before and after implementing a new recruitment strategy.

Business Knowledge:

- Apply principles from various business disciplines to improve HR practices.
- Example: Utilize marketing principles to develop an employer branding campaign.

Leveraging Technology:

- Utilize HRIS and business tools to solve HR-related problems.
- Example: Use HRIS data to identify trends in employee turnover.

Proficiency Indicators:

All HR Professionals:

- Data analysis is used to inform HR decisions and program design.
- Apply knowledge of business principles to enhance internal HR functions.
- Utilize HRIS and business technology to solve problems and address HR needs.

Advanced HR Professionals:

- Design and evaluate HR initiatives considering factors like ROI and profitability.
- Conduct risk assessments to inform HR strategy.
- Use HRIS and business technology to solve complex business problems impacting HR.

Importance:

Business analysis equips HR professionals to:

- Make data-driven decisions supporting business objectives.
- Design effective HR programs delivering measurable results.
- Demonstrate the financial impact of HR initiatives on the organization.

Behavioral Competency - Business Acumen

Sub-Competency

(C) Strategic Alignment

- **Definition:** Utilize business analysis tools to inform HR strategies.

Key Responsibilities:

Responsibility	Description	Example
Understanding the Big Picture	Grasp the connection between effective HR and core business functions.	Developing a training program for salespeople to improve sales performance.
Aligned Decision-Making	Make choices that align with HR's strategic direction and the organization's goals.	Recruiting strategy aligned with business expansion goals.
Building the Business Case	Develop strong arguments (including data) to demonstrate the value and ROI of HR initiatives.	Demonstrating ROI of an employee retention program by analyzing cost savings from turnover.

Proficiency Indicators:

Proficiency Level	Indicators
All HR Professionals	- Understand how effective HR practices contribute to successful business functions. Ensure HR decisions align with the organization's strategic direction and goals. Develop and present persuasive business cases for HR initiatives, showcasing their impact on efficiency and effectiveness.
Advanced HR Professionals	- Clearly articulate HR and organizational strategy, goals, and challenges in terms of business outcomes. Align HR's strategic direction and long-term goals with the overall business strategy of the organization. Act as strategic advisors, actively participating in organizational decision-making across various domains.

Importance:

Strategic alignment ensures HR initiatives contribute strategically to achieving organizational goals, resulting in:

- Improved Business Performance.
- Demonstrated HR Value.
- Stronger Collaboration between HR and business leaders.

Quiz Corner 7 - Business Acumen

Stand-alone Knowledge-Based Questions:

1. A key performance indicator (KPI) used to track employee engagement is:

a. Turnover rate
b. Cost per hire
c. Customer satisfaction score
d. Employee Net Promoter Score

2) A company analyzing its strengths, weaknesses, opportunities, and threats (SWOT) is primarily focused on understanding its:

a. Financial performance
b. Internal processes
c. Competitive landscape and external environment
d. Legal compliance requirements

3) A balanced scorecard is a management tool that uses metrics beyond financial measures to track performance across various areas. Which of the following is NOT typically included in a balanced scorecard?

a. Customer satisfaction
b. Employee engagement
c. Cash flow
d. Learning and growth

4) A company experiencing a surge in demand for its products might need to adjust its HR practices by:

a. Implementing a hiring freeze
b. Increasing training and development programs to upskill the workforce
c. Reducing employee benefits
d. Enforcing stricter performance management processes

5) Which of the following is an example of a fixed cost in an organization's budget?

a. Raw materials used in production
b. Rent for office space
c. Sales commissions
d. Travel expenses for salespeople

Quiz Corner 7 - Business Acumen

Stand-alone Knowledge-Based Questions:

6. The return on investment (ROI) for an HR initiative helps to measure:

a. Employee satisfaction with the program
b. The financial benefit of the program in relation to its cost
c. The time it takes to implement the program
d. The ease of use of the program for HR professionals

7. A service level agreement (SLA) outlines the expected level of service for a particular service provided within an organization. An example of an SLA in HR could be:

a. Guidelines for employee conduct
b. Performance expectations for a specific job role
c. Agreement between HR and IT regarding the time it takes to resolve employee IT issues
d. Standards for onboarding new employees (An onboarding program more likely covers this.)
.

8. Which of the following is NOT a core competency of Business Analysis within the SHRM Business Acumen sub-competency?

a. Conducting cost-benefit analysis of HR programs
b. Understanding legal implications of HR policies
c. Developing strong communication skills
d. Utilizing HR information systems (HRIS) to analyze data

9. When presenting a business case for an HR initiative, it's essential to demonstrate:

a. The complexity of the program design
b. Alignment with the organization's strategic goals and potential benefits
c. The specific HR technology tools needed for implementation
d. The time required for HR professionals to implement the program

10) Which of the following ratios might a company use to assess its profitability when analyzing its financial statements?
a. Current ratio
b. Debt-to-equity ratio
c. Price-to-earnings ratio
d. Profit margin

Quiz Corner 7 - Business Acumen

Scenario-Based Situational Judgment Questions:

1. You are the HR business partner for a manufacturing company facing a skills gap in a critical area. The company hesitates to invest in training current employees due to concerns about the time and cost involved. What is the BEST course of action?

Question:

Which of the following actions would be MOST appropriate in this situation?

a. Develop a cost-benefit analysis showcasing the long-term benefits of upskilling the workforce.
b. Focus on recruiting new talent with the required skills.
c. Reduce workload for existing employees to avoid the need for additional skills.
d. Offer voluntary buyout packages to encourage early retirement of senior employees.

2. The CEO announces a company-wide initiative to improve customer service. As the HR Manager, you know some customer service representatives are unhappy with their current workload and compensation. What should you do as a FIRST step?

a. Develop and implement a new customer service training program.
b. Focus on internal communication to ensure everyone understands the CEO's vision.
c. Conduct employee surveys or focus groups to understand employee concerns about customer service.
d. Partner with the marketing department to develop new customer service messaging.

3. A new law that impacts your company's employee benefits program goes into effect. What is the MOST crucial action to take first?

a. Update all HR policies and procedures to reflect the new law.
b. Conduct training sessions for HR professionals on the new law's implications.
c. Consult with an employment lawyer to understand the new law's specific requirements for your company.
d. Communicate the changes to employees through a company-wide announcement.

4. A high-performing employee approaches you and expresses frustration about the company's lack of growth opportunities. What is the BEST way to respond?

a. Encourage the employee to participate in more company-sponsored social events.
b. Reassure the employee that their hard work is appreciated and there are opportunities for advancement in the future.
c. Schedule a meeting to discuss the employee's career goals and explore potential development opportunities within the company.
d. Advise the employee to update their resume and look for opportunities elsewhere.

5. Your company is undergoing a merger with another company. Employees from both companies are anxious about potential job losses and changes to company culture. How can HR MOST effectively address these concerns?

a. Focus on the merger's potential benefits, such as increased market share.
b. Wait until all decisions are finalized before communicating anything to employees.
c. Organize open forum sessions to address employee questions and concerns in a transparent manner.
d. Develop a detailed communication plan to outline the merger process and keep employees informed at every stage.

Quiz Corner 7 - Business Acumen

Scenario-Based Situational Judgment Questions:

6. An employee approaches you and expresses concerns about a colleague's inappropriate behavior. The behavior is not discriminatory or harassing but creates a tense work environment. What should you do first?

a. Ask the employee to provide specific examples of the behavior and document the conversation.
b. Confront the colleague directly and explain how their behavior affects the workplace.
c. Encourage the employee to ignore the behavior and focus on their own work.
d. Refer the employee to the company's Employee Assistance Program (EAP) for support.

7. A new manager has joined the company and seems hesitant to delegate tasks to their team members. This is causing a bottleneck and impacting team productivity. How can HR MOST effectively address this issue?

a. Publicly criticize the manager for their lack of delegation skills.
b. Offer the manager additional training on leadership and delegation.
c. Schedule a private meeting with the manager to discuss the importance of delegation and its impact on team performance.
d. Reassign some of the manager's tasks to other team members to alleviate bottlenecks.

8. During the annual performance review process, an employee receives a lower rating than expected and expresses disagreement with the feedback. What is the BEST course of action for the HR professional?

a. Side with the manager, who provided the feedback and advised the employee to accept the rating.
b. Reassure the employee and suggest they focus on improving areas identified in the feedback.
c. Facilitate a discussion between the employee and their manager to discuss the feedback and ensure understanding.
d. Change the employee's performance rating to avoid any potential conflict.

9. The company is planning a large-scale company picnic. You notice a group of employees who seem excluded from social events. How can HR MOST effectively promote inclusivity?

a. Provide a list of attendees to all employees beforehand.
b. Organize more minor team-building activities throughout the year instead of a significant event.
c. Encourage employee participation in planning the picnic and ensure activities cater to diverse interests.
d. Offer alternative activities for employees not interested in attending the picnic.

10. A key employee announces their resignation to pursue another opportunity. Their departure will create a significant knowledge gap within the team. What steps should HR take first?

- a. Immediately begin recruiting for a replacement to fill the vacant position.
- b. Offer the employee a counteroffer to convince them to stay with the company.
- c. Schedule a meeting with the departing employee to understand their reasons for leaving and discuss knowledge transfer opportunities.
- d. Announce the vacancy to the team and encourage internal applications.

Quiz Corner 7 - Business Acumen

Stand-alone Knowledge-Based Questions:

1. d. Employee Net Promoter Score
2. c. Competitive landscape and external environment
3. c. Cash flow
4. b. Increasing training and development programs to upskill the workforce
5. b. Rent for office space
6. b. The financial benefit of the program in relation to its cost
7. c. Agreement between HR and IT regarding the time it takes to resolve employee IT issues
8. a. Conducting cost-benefit analysis of HR programs
9. b. Alignment with the organization's strategic goals and potential benefits
10. d. Profit margin

Scenario-Based Situational Judgment Questions:

1. a. Develop a cost-benefit analysis showcasing the long-term benefits of upskilling the workforce. (This directly addresses the company's concerns and demonstrates the value of training.)
2. c. Conduct employee surveys or focus groups to understand employee concerns about customer service. (**This is the BEST first step to gather information and identify areas for improvement.**)
3. c. Consult with an employment lawyer to understand the new law's specific requirements for your company. (**This is the MOST important first step to ensure legal compliance.**)
4. c. Schedule a meeting to discuss the employee's career goals and explore potential development opportunities within the company. (**This is the BEST approach to address the employee's concerns and retain talent.**)
5. c. Organize open forum sessions to address employee questions and concerns in a transparent manner. (**This is the MOST effective approach to build trust and manage anxiety.**)
6. a. Ask the employee to provide specific examples of the behavior and document the conversation. (**This is a good first step to gather information.**)
7. c. Schedule a private meeting with the manager to discuss the importance of delegation and its impact on team performance. (**This is a more direct and constructive approach.**)
8. c. Facilitate a discussion between the employee and their manager to discuss the feedback and ensure understanding. (**This allows for open communication and helps resolve the disagreement.**)
9. c. Encourage employee participation in planning the picnic and ensure activities cater to diverse interests. (**This promotes ownership and inclusivity.**)
10. c. Schedule a meeting with the departing employee to understand their reasons for leaving and discuss knowledge transfer opportunities. (**This prioritizes capturing their knowledge and ensures a smoother transition.**)

Behavioral Competency - (2) Consultation

Collaboration with stakeholders to address business challenges and implement effective HR solutions.

Sub-competencies

Sub-competency	Explanation	Example
Evaluating Business Challenges	Analyze complex issues to determine HR's role in solutions.	Assessing the impact of organizational restructuring on employee morale.
Designing HR Solutions	Develop effective HR strategies and programs addressing business needs.	Creating flexible work policies for improved work-life balance.
Advising on HR Solutions	Provide expert guidance on HR practices to stakeholders.	Advising on talent acquisition strategies to attract top talent.
Change Management	Effectively manage HR-related changes within the organization.	Leading a team through the implementation of a new performance management system.
Service Excellence	Deliver exceptional HR services to internal clients.	Providing personalized training sessions based on employee needs.

Key Concepts & Examples

Organizational Change Management

Theories and Models:

Theory/Model	Definition	Example
Lewin's Change Management Model	A three-stage model (Unfreeze, Change, Refreeze) emphasizing the need to first unfreeze existing behaviors before making changes.	Implementing a new performance appraisal system involves unfreezing old appraisal practices.

Theory/Model	Definition	Example
McKinsey 7S Model	Analyzes seven key elements (Strategy, Structure, Systems, Shared Values, Skills, Style, Staff) to understand their interrelation.	Analyzing how changes in strategy impact organizational structure and employee skills.
Kotter's 8-Step Change Model	Provides a step-by-step approach for leading organizational change.	Leading a change initiative by establishing a sense of urgency among employees.
Kubler-Ross Change Curve	Describes the emotional stages individuals go through during change (Denial, Anger, Bargaining, Depression, Acceptance).	Recognizing and addressing employees' resistance to change during a restructuring process.

Change Management Processes:

Process	Description	Example
Obtaining Leadership Buy-In	Secure support from key leaders to champion the change initiative.	Gaining support from top management for implementing a new HRIS system.
Building a Case for Change	Gather data and evidence to demonstrate the need for change.	Presenting findings from employee surveys to justify the implementation of a wellness program.
Engaging Employees	Actively involve employees in the change process.	Hosting focus groups to gather input from employees on redesigning the performance management system.
Communicating Change	Clearly communicate change to all stakeholders.	Holding town hall meetings to announce upcoming organizational changes and address concerns.
Removing Barriers	Identify and address obstacles hindering change implementation.	Conducting training sessions to address skill gaps hindering the adoption of new technology.

Remember

- Strong interpersonal skills are crucial.
- Adapt approach to specific challenges and clients.
- Continuous learning is essential.

Behavioral Competency - Consultation

Sub-Competency

(A) Evaluating Business Challenges

Definition: This sub-competency emphasizes identifying business challenges and potential HR solutions in collaboration with stakeholders. HR professionals must grasp the broader organizational context and how HR can enhance overall success.

Proficiency Indicators:

For All HR Professionals:

Indicator	Example
Partners with stakeholders	- Regularly meets with business leaders and department heads to discuss challenges and priorities. - Conducts surveys or focus groups to gather employee feedback.
Understands current & future challenges	- Analyzes HR data (e.g., turnover rates) to identify potential issues. - Stays updated on industry trends impacting the organization's workforce.
Identifies HR needs & opportunities	- Recognizes situations for HR practices to improve efficiency or engagement. - Identifies skill gaps and proposes relevant training programs.
Informs stakeholders about HR threats	- Alerts stakeholders about legal risks with current HR practices. - Provides insights on upcoming legislative changes affecting HR policies.
Advises on existing HR programs	- Evaluates HR program effectiveness and suggests improvements. - Recommends adjustments to existing policies hindering business goals.

Proficiency Indicators:

For Advanced HR Professionals:

Indicator	Example
Improves business outcomes	- Analyzes data to correlate HR practices with key business metrics (e.g., employee engagement and customer satisfaction). - Develops HR strategies for organizational goals.
Supports strategic direction	- Collaborates with leadership to understand long-term vision. - Proposes HR initiatives aligning with strategic direction.

Tips for Success:

- Develop strong communication skills to build trust with stakeholders.
- Stay updated on HR trends to identify improvement opportunities.
- Utilize data analytics to support potential HR solutions.
- Think strategically for long-term organizational impact.

By mastering these skills, you demonstrate value as a business partner and contribute to organizational success.

Behavioral Competency - Consultation

Sub-Competency

(B)Designing HR Solutions

Definition: Focuses on developing effective HR strategies and programs aligned with business needs.

Proficiency Indicators:

For All HR Professionals:

Indicator	Example
Partnering for Solutions	- Collaborate with business partners and legal departments to ensure compliance and alignment. - Engage HR subject matter experts for best practice insights.
Creativity & Innovation	- Propose innovative solutions tailored to organizational needs. - Explore non-traditional HR approaches. - Adapt successful practices from similar industries.
Effectiveness & Best Practices	- Base solutions on data and industry best practices. - Assess potential ROI and impact. - Benchmark against industry standards.
Defining Goals & Outcomes	- Establish clear, measurable goals and KPIs. - Communicate expected outcomes to stakeholders.

For Advanced HR Professionals:

Indicator	Example
Minimizing Threats & Liabilities	- Analyze data to identify HR risks and propose mitigation strategies. - Develop contingency plans for legal compliance.
Strategic Remediation	- Prioritize actions to address HR threats. - Adapt strategies as needed.
Talent Management Strategies	- Design evidence-based talent management plans aligned with business strategy. - Use analytics to identify talent gaps and develop solutions.
Long-Term HR & Business Solutions	- Oversee strategic HR plans supporting organizational growth. - Integrate HR initiatives with business planning. - Continuously refine solutions based on data and evolving needs.

Proficiency Indicators:

For All HR Professionals:

Indicator	Example
Partnering for Solutions	- Collaborate with business partners and legal departments to ensure compliance and alignment. - Engage HR subject matter experts for best practice insights.
Creativity & Innovation	- Propose innovative solutions tailored to organizational needs. - Explore non-traditional HR approaches. - Adapt successful practices from similar industries.
Effectiveness & Best Practices	- Base solutions on data and industry best practices. - Assess potential ROI and impact. - Benchmark against industry standards.
Defining Goals & Outcomes	- Establish clear, measurable goals and KPIs. - Communicate expected outcomes to stakeholders.

For Advanced HR Professionals:

Indicator	Example
Minimizing Threats & Liabilities	- Analyze data to identify HR risks and propose mitigation strategies. - Develop contingency plans for legal compliance.
Strategic Remediation	- Prioritize actions to address HR threats. - Adapt strategies as needed.
Talent Management Strategies	- Design evidence-based talent management plans aligned with business strategy. - Use analytics to identify talent gaps and develop solutions.
Long-Term HR & Business Solutions	- Oversee strategic HR plans supporting organizational growth. - Integrate HR initiatives with business planning. - Continuously refine solutions based on data and evolving needs.

Tips for Success:

- Develop problem-solving skills for complex challenges.
- Stay updated on HR trends and best practices.
- Master data analysis for solution effectiveness.
- Build strong stakeholder relationships for support.

Behavioral Competency - Consultation

Sub-Competency

(C) Advising on HR Solutions

Definition: Focuses on guiding stakeholders in HR solution implementation.

Proficiency Indicators:

For All HR Professionals:

Indicator	Example
Provide Guidance	- Offer training and support on new HR programs. - Develop clear communication materials and FAQs. - Facilitate workshops for stakeholder skill-building.
Overcome Obstacles	- Collaborate to address implementation roadblocks. - Propose alternative solutions for challenges.
Follow-up & Support	- Monitor implementation progress. - Gather stakeholder feedback for improvement. - Address concerns promptly.
Ensure Goal Alignment	- Track KPIs for solution effectiveness. - Analyze data for goal alignment. - Adjust programs as needed.

Tips for Success:

- Develop communication skills for stakeholder trust.
- Master the HR solution for practical guidance.
- Build relationships for support and buy-in.
- Anticipate challenges and solve them proactively.

Mastering these skills demonstrates your value as a trusted advisor in HR solution implementation.

Proficiency Indicators:
For Advanced HR Professionals:

Indicator	Example
Strategic Support	- Provide tailored HR solutions aligned with strategic goals. - Stay updated on industry trends for future success.
Encourage Input	- Create feedback channels for employee and leader input. - Integrate feedback into HR solution design.
Overcome Implementation Obstacles	- Anticipate challenges for strategic HR initiatives. - Develop contingency plans for smooth implementation.
Integrate Solutions	- Ensure seamless integration of HR solutions with organizational processes. - Identify synergies with other departments. - Foster cross-departmental collaboration for effectiveness.

Behavioral Competency - Consultation

Sub-Competency

(D) Change Management

Definition: This sub-competency evaluates your ability to navigate and support organizational change initiatives, which is pivotal in promoting buy-in and overseeing successful implementation.

Proficiency Indicators:

Level	Indicator	Example
All HR Professionals	Recommend Improvements	- Analyze data for HR program enhancements. - Propose evidence-based changes (e.g., recruitment strategy updates for diversity).

Level	Indicator	Example
All HR Professionals	Promote Stakeholder Buy-in	- Develop clear communication plans. - Address concerns transparently. - Involve stakeholders in the change process (e.g., surveys).
All HR Professionals	Build Staff Buy-in	- Foster open communication culture. - Highlight positive change impact (e.g., flexible work policy). - Recognize supportive employees.
All HR Professionals	Align HR Programs	- Review and adjust HR programs to support change goals. - Develop new resources if necessary.
Advanced HR Professionals	Identify Change Needs	- Analyze data and trends for necessary changes. - Recommend proactive initiatives.
Advanced HR Professionals	Lead Buy-in at All Levels	- Develop comprehensive communication strategies. - Secure leadership buy-in. - Tailor messaging for various stakeholders.
Advanced HR Professionals	Define Objectives & Goals	- Collaborate on clear objectives aligned with strategy. - Establish measurable goals and KPIs.
Advanced HR Professionals	Oversee Implementation	- Develop detailed implementation plans. - Collaborate with business units for smooth execution. - Address obstacles promptly.
Advanced HR Professionals	Partner with Business Leaders	- Build strong relationships with leaders. - Provide guidance and support throughout change. - Address challenges collaboratively.
Advanced HR Professionals	Support HR Staff	- Provide training and resources for HR staff. - Foster supportive environment. - Recognize outstanding contributions.

Tips for Success:

- Develop communication and interpersonal skills.
- Familiarize with change management models.
- Build relationships at all levels.
- Be proactive and anticipate challenges.

Mastering these skills demonstrates your value as a change management resource.

Behavioral Competency - Consultation

Sub-Competency

(E) Service Excellence

Definition: Focuses on delivering exceptional HR services and fostering a customer service culture within the HR department.

Proficiency Indicators:

Level	Indicator	Example
All HR Professionals	Identify Stakeholder Needs	- Actively listen to stakeholders through surveys or meetings. - Analyze HR data for service improvement opportunities.
All HR Professionals	Responsive Communication	- Respond promptly and courteously to stakeholder inquiries. - Communicate transparently throughout the process.
All HR Professionals	Proactive Problem Solving	- Anticipate service delivery risks and develop contingency plans. - Address dissatisfaction signs proactively.
All HR Professionals	Vendor Management	- Maintain positive relationships with HR vendors. - Monitor and communicate vendor performance effectively.
Advanced HR Professionals	Design for Service Excellence	- Develop HR programs prioritizing stakeholder service. - Implement technology solutions for efficient service delivery.
Advanced HR Professionals	Oversee Service Objectives	- Set clear service objectives and measure outcomes. - Hold HR staff accountable for service quality.
Advanced HR Professionals	Identify System Needs	- Analyze organizational systems affecting service. - Collaborate with stakeholders to address service-related issues.
Advanced HR Professionals	Build a Service Culture	- Promote a service-oriented culture within HR. - Recognize and reward high-quality service provision.

Quiz Corner 8 - Consultation

Stand-alone Knowledge-Based Questions:

1. Which change management model emphasizes the importance of unfreezing the current state, transitioning to a new state, and refreezing to make the change permanent?

A. McKinsey 7S Framework
B. Kubler-Ross Change Curve
C. Lewin's Change Management Model
D. Kotter's 8-Step Change Model

2) When consulting with stakeholders, what is an essential technique to ensure successful client interactions?

A. Avoiding eye contact to project confidence
B. Listening actively and demonstrating empathy
C. Focusing on technical jargon to showcase expertise
D. Sharing personal opinions about the situation

3) Which of the following is NOT a key component of designing HR solutions?

A. Partnering with stakeholders to identify needs
B. Basing solutions on best practices and research
C. Defining clear goals and expected outcomes
D. Implementing the solution without stakeholder input

4) When advising on HR solutions, what should an HR professional prioritize to ensure successful implementation?

A. Delegating all tasks to non-HR managers
B. Providing ongoing support and guidance to stakeholders
C. Rushing through the implementation process
D. Ignoring feedback or concerns raised by stakeholders

5) What is the primary objective of service excellence in the HR context?

A. Reducing the workload of HR professionals
B. Providing high-quality service to all stakeholders
C. Focusing solely on internal HR processes
D. Minimizing interaction with external vendors

Quiz Corner 8 - Consultation

Scenario-Based Situational Judgment Questions:

1. You are the HR Business Partner for the Marketing department. The Marketing Director approaches you, concerned about a recent spike in employee turnover. They believe the current compensation structure is no longer competitive, leading to employees leaving for better-paying opportunities. What is the BEST course of action?

A. Agree with the Marketing Director and immediately recommend a pay raise for the entire department.
B. Explain to the Marketing Director that you cannot address compensation concerns and suggest they speak to finance.
C. Gather data on industry compensation trends for similar roles and conduct a preliminary analysis to present to the Marketing Director.
D. Tell the Marketing Director you'll look into it but prioritize other more pressing HR matters.

2. You are leading the organization's implementation of a new performance management system. Some managers have expressed concerns about the system's complexity and the additional time it requires to complete performance reviews. How should you address these concerns?

- A. Remind managers that the new system is mandatory and there is no room for negotiation.
- B. Offer additional training sessions on using the new system but dismiss their concerns about time commitment.
- C. Work with managers to identify specific areas of difficulty with the new system and explore potential solutions to streamline the process.
- D. Delegate responsibility for addressing these concerns to a junior HR staff member.

3. You are consulting with the CEO on potential solutions to address a skills gap within the organization that is hindering innovation. You recommend developing a comprehensive training and development program. The CEO expresses concerns about the budget and suggests hiring externally to fill the skills gap. How should you respond?

- A. Accept the CEO's decision and focus on recruitment efforts.
- B. Explain the benefits of training existing employees and present data on the cost-effectiveness of internal talent development compared to external recruitment.
- C. Tell the CEO you strongly disagree and insist on implementing the training program regardless of budget constraints.
- D. Defer to the CEO's decision and avoid further discussion.

4. A new company policy regarding flexible work arrangements has been implemented. However, you receive several complaints from employees who feel their managers are not somewhat approving requests for flexible work schedules. How should you handle this situation?

A. Ignore the complaints, as some employees will always resist change.
B. Hold a mandatory training session for all managers on the new flexible work policy, emphasizing fairness in approvals.
C. Publicly reprimand managers who have denied flexible work requests.
D. Tell the employees nothing you can do, and the manager's decisions are final.

5. You are the HR Consultant for a large manufacturing plant. The plant manager is concerned about a recent decline in employee morale and productivity. They suspect a communication gap exists between management and employees. How should you approach this situation?

A. Recommend a company-wide employee satisfaction survey without involving management in planning.
B. Tell the plant manager it's their responsibility to improve communication with employees and offer no further assistance.
C. Schedule one-on-one meetings with a few disgruntled employees to gather their specific concerns.
D. Facilitate a joint meeting with the plant manager and employee representatives to discuss communication challenges and develop solutions collaboratively.

Quiz Corner 8 - Consultation

Stand-alone Knowledge-Based Questions:

1. C. Lewin's Change Management Model
2. B. Listening actively and demonstrating empathy
3. B. Basing solutions on best practices and research
4. B. Providing ongoing support and guidance to stakeholders
5. B. Providing high-quality service to all stakeholders

Scenario-Based Situational Judgment Questions:

1. C. Gather data on industry compensation trends for similar roles and conduct a preliminary analysis to present to the Marketing Director. (Correct Answer - This demonstrates data-driven decision-making and collaboration)
2. C. Work with managers to identify specific areas of difficulty with the new system and explore potential solutions to streamline the process. (Correct Answer - This demonstrates active listening and problem-solving)
3. B. Explain the benefits of training existing employees and present data on the cost-effectiveness of internal talent development compared to external recruitment. (Correct Answer - Provides data-driven justification for your recommendation)
4. B. Hold a mandatory training session for all managers on the new flexible work policy, emphasizing fairness in approvals. (Correct Answer - This provides targeted education to address the root cause)
5. D. Facilitate a joint meeting with the plant manager and employee representatives to discuss communication challenges and develop solutions collaboratively. (Correct Answer - Encourages open communication and collaboration)

Behavioral Competency - (3) Analytical Aptitude

It focuses on your ability to effectively work with data to assess HR initiatives, inform business decisions, and make evidence-based recommendations.

Sub-competencies:

Sub-competency	Description
Data Advocate	- Champion the use of data for HR decisions. - Educate stakeholders on the importance of data-driven decision making.
Data Gathering	- Select appropriate data sources for HR questions. - Design effective data collection methods.
Data Analysis	- Clean, organize, and prepare data. - Apply analysis techniques to extract insights.
Evidence-Based Decision-Making	- Use data to support HR recommendations. - Communicate insights clearly to stakeholders.

Key Concepts:

Survey and Assessment Processes:

- Understand survey and assessment development, administration, and validation.

Data Sources:

- Interviews, Focus Groups, Employee Surveys, Customer Surveys, Marketing Data, Analytical Reports.

Data Analysis Techniques:

- Data Cleansing, Data Mining, Data Visualization, Big Data Analysis, Statistical Analysis, Predictive Analytics.

Basic Statistics & Measurement:
- Descriptive Statistics, Correlation, Reliability, Validity.

Graph & Chart Interpretation:
- Interpret and conclude from graphs and charts.

Data for Business Cases:
- Utilize data to support HR initiatives.

Tips for Success:

- Develop strong analytical thinking skills.
- Gain proficiency in fundamental statistical analysis and data visualization techniques.
- Understand HR metrics and their interpretation.
- Practice clear and concise communication of data-driven insights.

Mastering these skills demonstrates the ability to leverage data strategically for HR decisions and organizational success.

Behavioral Competency - Analytical Aptitude

Sub-Competency

(A) Data Advocate

- **Definition:** Assess the ability to champion data-driven decision-making in HR and across the organization.

Proficiency Indicators:

All HR Professionals:
- Advocate for data use in evaluating HR programs.
- Encourage evidence-based decisions.

- Emphasize program validation.
- Identify data-driven decision points.

Advanced HR Professionals:

- Link HR data to strategic goals.
- Promote a data-driven culture.
- Utilize HR metrics.
- Ensure data-driven HR functions.

Benefit	Description	Example
Improved Program Effectiveness	Data identifies strengths and weaknesses for targeted improvements.	Analyzing training data reveals knowledge gaps, prompting curriculum adjustments.
Reduced Costs	Data optimization minimizes HR-related costs.	Identifying high-risk talent flight enables targeted retention strategies.
Enhanced Talent Management	Data insights into employee engagement and development needs.	Performance data helps identify high-potential employees for leadership development.
Stronger Business Alignment	HR initiatives align strategically with overall business goals.	Workforce demographics guide talent acquisition strategies supporting new business ventures.

Tips for Success:

- Understand HR data value and limitations.
- Stay updated on HR analytics trends.
- Communicate data insights effectively.
- Partner with data analysts and stakeholders.

Championing data-driven decisions demonstrates the ability to contribute to a strategic and evidence-based HR function.

Behavioral Competency - Analytical Aptitude

Sub-Competency

(B) Data Gathering

- **Definition:** Assess the ability to identify and collect relevant data to inform HR decisions and initiatives.

Proficiency Indicators:

All HR Professionals:
- Maintain an understanding of data collection methods and HR metrics.
- Identify relevant data sources and utilize internal and external data.
- Select appropriate data collection methods and scan external sources.
- Benchmark HR initiatives against industry standards.

Advanced HR Professionals:
- Advocate for systematic data collection processes.
- Stay updated on emerging data collection methods and technologies.
- Collaborate externally to gain access to relevant HR data.

Method	Description	Advantages	Disadvantages
Surveys	Questionnaires administered to a sample population.	Efficient for large data collection.	Low response rates, potential bias, and data quality concerns.
Interviews	In-depth conversations with individuals.	Provides rich qualitative data.	Time-consuming and resource-intensive.
Focus Groups	Moderated discussions with a small group of people.	Explores diverse perspectives and ideas.	Group dynamics may influence participation.
Existing Data Analysis	Extracting data from internal HR systems and reports.	Provides readily available data.	Data may lack comprehensiveness or relevance.
External Data Sources	Industry reports, government statistics, labor market data.	Provides broader context and insights.	Requires careful evaluation for quality and relevance.

Tips for Success:

- Clearly understand the HR question or problem.
- Identify relevant data sources.
- Select appropriate data collection methods.
- Design data collection tools effectively.
- Ensure reliability and validity of data collection methods.

Mastering these skills enables informed HR decisions, leading to a successful HR function.

Behavioral Competency - Analytical Aptitude

Sub-Competency

(C) Data Analysis

- **Definition:** Assess the ability to analyze and interpret data for HR decision-making and program evaluation.

Proficiency Indicators:

All HR Professionals:

- Maintain an understanding of statistical concepts and data analysis techniques.
- Identify data flaws and conduct fundamental data analysis for meaningful insights.
- Maintain objectivity and identify data gaps.

Advanced HR Professionals:

- Possess a deeper understanding of advanced statistical concepts.
- Lead comprehensive evaluations of HR programs.
- Critically review data analysis results and translate findings into recommendations.

Technique	Description	Example
Descriptive Statistics	Summarize key data characteristics (e.g., mean, median, standard deviation).	Calculating average time-to-hire for new employees across departments.
Hypothesis Testing	Test hypotheses about variable relationships.	Testing if a new training program leads to higher employee engagement scores.
Correlation Analysis	Measure strength and direction of variable relationships.	Analyzing correlation between employee satisfaction and retention rates.
Trend Analysis	Identify patterns and trends in data over time.	Examining recruitment cost trends over the past year.
Regression Analysis	Predict future outcomes based on variable relationships.	Modeling impact of compensation levels on employee turnover.

Tips for Success:

- Clearly understand the HR question or problem.
- Choose appropriate data analysis techniques.
- Clean and prepare data for accurate analysis.
- Utilize data visualization tools for effective communication.
- Maintain objectivity throughout the analysis process.

Mastering these skills enables valuable insights, program evaluations, and informed HR decisions.

Behavioral Competency - Analytical Aptitude

Sub-Competency

(D) Evidence-Based Decision-Making

- **Definition:** Assess ability to use data analysis findings for strategic HR decisions and practices.

Proficiency Indicators:

All HR Professionals:

- Effectively communicate data analysis findings.
- Utilize research findings to evaluate options.
- Transfer knowledge and adapt practices based on evidence.

Advanced HR Professionals:

- Communicate critical findings and implications to senior leaders.
- Develop evidence-based HR strategies.
- Champion process improvement initiatives.

Benefit	Description	Example
Improved Decision Making	Data-driven insights lead to informed HR decisions.	Analyzing employee turnover data reveals high turnover rates in a department, prompting targeted retention strategies.
Reduced Costs	Data identifies areas for cost savings and resource optimization.	Analyzing recruitment data highlights interview process inefficiencies, leading to cost savings through process improvement.
Enhanced Program Effectiveness	Evidence-based practices ensure HR programs align with employee needs and deliver desired outcomes.	Analyzing training program data prompts adjustments in curriculum design for improved effectiveness.
Stronger Alignment with Business Strategy	HR initiatives are strategically linked to overall business goals through data.	Analyzing workforce demographics informs talent acquisition strategies to support emerging business ventures.

Tips for Success:

- Develop strong communication skills for presenting data findings.
- Stay updated on HR research and best practices.
- Cultivate critical thinking for objective data evaluation.
- Collaborate with data analysts for effective data utilization.

Quiz Corner 9 - Analytical Aptitude

Stand-alone Knowledge-Based Questions:

1. Which of the following is NOT a source of data for HR analysis?

A. Employee surveys
B. Exit interviews
C. Government reports
D. Customer satisfaction surveys

2) When interpreting a scatterplot, what does a positive correlation between two variables indicate?

A. There is no relationship between the variables.
B. As one variable increases, the other variable tends to decrease.
C. The data points are randomly scattered with no pattern.
D. It is impossible to determine the relationship without additional information.

3) Which data analysis technique is used to identify trends and patterns in data over time?

A. Hypothesis testing
B. Regression analysis
C. Trend analysis
D. Reliability analysis

4) What is the primary benefit of using data visualization tools (e.g., charts, graphs) in HR analysis?

A. To perform complex statistical calculations.
B. To simplify the data collection process.
C. To effectively communicate data insights to stakeholders.
D. To ensure the accuracy and completeness of data sets.

5) Which of the following statements is MOST aligned with the concept of evidence-based decision-making in HR?

A. Relying solely on personal experience and intuition when making HR decisions.
B. Basing HR decisions on industry trends without considering internal data.
C. Utilizing data analysis findings to support and justify HR recommendations.
D. Implementing HR programs solely based on their popularity within the organization.

Quiz Corner 9 - Analytical Aptitude

Scenario-Based Situational Judgment Questions:

1. You are the HR Manager for a large retail company. Sales performance has been declining recently, and senior leadership suspects low employee morale might be a contributing factor. What is the BEST course of action to gather data relevant to this situation?

- A. Conduct a focus group with a small sample of employees from different departments.
- B. Analyze existing sales data to identify trends and potential correlations.
- C. Implement a company-wide employee survey to gauge employee satisfaction and engagement.
- D. Review recent disciplinary records to identify any patterns of employee misconduct.

2. Your company's HR department recently implemented a new training program for managers on effective performance management techniques. However, you receive feedback from some employees who feel their managers are still not providing constructive feedback during performance reviews. How should you approach this situation?

A. Ignore the feedback, assuming it only represents a few disgruntled employees.
B. Conduct additional training sessions for managers on the importance of providing feedback.
C. Analyze data from employee performance reviews to identify potential inconsistencies in feedback practices.
D. Ask the complaining employees to provide specific examples of their concerns but take no further action.

3. You are the HR Business Partner for the Marketing department. The Marketing Director approaches you, concerned about a recent spike in employee turnover. They believe the current workload is unsustainable and leads to burnout among employees. What is the BEST course of action?

A. Immediately approve the Marketing Director's request to hire additional staff.
B. Conduct exit interviews with departing employees to understand their reasons for leaving.
C. Analyze workload distribution data for the Marketing team to identify potential imbalances.
D. Recommend a company-wide wellness program to improve employee morale.

4 . You are the HR Analyst for a manufacturing company. The company is considering implementing a new wellness program to improve employee health and reduce healthcare costs. Management is asking for your input on how to evaluate the program's effectiveness. What is the BEST approach?

A. Conduct a company-wide survey before and after the program to gauge employee health perceptions.
B. Track healthcare cost trends over time to see if there is a correlation with the program implementation.
C. Develop a balanced scorecard that includes metrics on program participation, employee health outcomes, and healthcare costs.
D. Focus solely on employee satisfaction surveys to measure the program's success.

5 . You are the HR Director for a rapidly growing technology company. You are concerned about effectively onboarding new hires and integrating them into the company culture. What data analysis would be most helpful in informing your recommendations?

A. Analyze time-to-hire data to identify areas for streamlining the recruitment process.
B. Conduct focus groups with current employees to gather their perspectives on company culture.
C. Track new hire turnover rates within the first 90 days of employment.
D. Analyze employee satisfaction surveys completed during the first month of employment.

Quiz Corner 9 - Analytical Aptitude

Stand-alone Knowledge-Based Questions:

1. B. Exit interviews (Correct Answer) - Exit interviews typically gather qualitative data for improvement purposes, not necessarily for analysis)
2. B. As one variable increases, the other variable tends to decrease. (Correct Answer)
3. C. Trend analysis (Correct Answer)
4. C. To effectively communicate data insights to stakeholders. (Correct Answer)
5. C. Utilizing data analysis findings to support and justify HR recommendations. (Correct Answer)

Scenario-Based Situational Judgment Questions:

1. C. Implement a company-wide employee survey to gauge employee satisfaction and engagement. (Correct Answer - Provides broader employee perspective)
2. C. Analyze data from employee performance reviews to identify potential inconsistencies in feedback practices. (Correct Answer - Data-driven approach to identify the scope of the issue)
3. C. Analyze workload distribution data for the Marketing team to identify potential imbalances. (Correct Answer - Data-driven approach to understand workload concerns)
4. C. Develop a balanced scorecard that includes metrics on program participation, employee health outcomes, and healthcare costs. (Correct Answer - Comprehensive approach that considers various factors)
5. C. Track new hire turnover rates within the first 90 days of employment. (Good indicator of onboarding effectiveness) (Correct Answer)

6. Domain 1: People Knowledge

Technical Competency

The HR Expertise competency is one technical competency which outlines **14 functional areas grouped into three domains.**

Domain 1: People Knowledge	Domain 2: Organizational Knowledge	Domain 3: Workplace Knowledge
HR Strategy	Structure of the HR Function	Managing a Global Workforce
Talent Acquisition	Organizational Effectiveness and Development	Risk Management
Employee Engagement and Retention	Workforce Management	Corporate Social Responsibility
Learning and Development	Employee Labor and Relations	US Employment Law and Regulations
Total Rewards	Technology Management	

HR professionals need a strong understanding of the People Knowledge Domain to manage people within an organization effectively. This domain covers five key functional areas:

- **HR Strategy**: Aligning HR practices with the organization's overall goals. (Example: Developing talent management programs to support future leadership needs)

- **Talent Acquisition**: Recruiting, selecting, and onboarding qualified employees. (Example: Utilizing job postings, assessments, and interview techniques to find the best candidate)

- **Employee Engagement & Retention**: Fostering a positive work environment that motivates employees to stay. (Example: Implementing recognition programs, offering competitive benefits, and providing growth opportunities)

- **Learning & Development**: Equipping employees with the skills and knowledge needed to succeed. (Example: Providing training programs, mentorship opportunities, and tuition reimbursement)

- **Total Rewards**: Designing a compensation and benefits package that attracts, retains, and motivates employees.

Component	Description	Example
Base Salary	Fixed monetary compensation	$75,000 annual salary
Bonus	Performance-based incentive pay	Up to 10% of base salary based on performance goals
Benefits	Non-cash compensation (health insurance, paid time off)	Health insurance, dental insurance, 20 days of paid vacation

Domain 1: People Knowledge

Functional Area : (A) HR Strategy

- **Definition:** HR Strategy is the cornerstone of effective human capital management. It aligns HR practices with organizational goals to maximize stakeholder value.

Project Management Approaches and Processes:

Approach	Description	Example
Traditional	Structured phases: initiating, planning, executing, monitoring, closing.	Implementing a new performance management system.
Lean Six Sigma	Focuses on continuous improvement, waste elimination.	Streamlining recruitment processes to reduce time-to-fill.
Agile	Adaptive, iterative approach with short development cycles.	Developing and launching a new employee feedback tool.

Approach	Description	Example
Critical Chain	Emphasizes resource management, buffer scheduling.	Allocating resources effectively for a training program.
Design Thinking	User-centered problem-solving and innovation approach.	Redesigning the onboarding process based on employee feedback.
Kaizen	Philosophy of continuous improvement through small, incremental changes.	Implementing daily huddles to address team challenges.

Project Management Processes:

Process	Description
Initiating	Defining project scope, objectives, stakeholders.
Planning and Designing	Developing detailed plans with timelines, resources, tasks.
Launching	Executing the project plan.
Monitoring and Controlling	Tracking progress, identifying risks, making adjustments.
Closing	Finalizing project, evaluating outcomes, documenting lessons learned.

Project Management Processes:

Tool	Description
Critical Path Analysis (CPA)	Identifies longest sequence of project activities needing completion on time.
Gantt Charts	Visualizes project timelines, dependencies.
Variance Analysis	Compares project performance against baselines, identifies deviations.
Outcome Monitoring	Tracks project results to assess achievement of objectives.

Project Leadership, Governance, and Structures:

Concept	Description
Team Roles	Different roles (e.g., project manager, subject matter expert) foster collaboration.
Team Management	Building trust, fostering communication, resolving conflicts are crucial leadership skills.
Work Breakdown Structures (WBS)	Breaking down projects into smaller, manageable tasks enhances planning, execution.

Systems Thinking in HR Strategy:

Concept	Description
Related Parts	HR strategy connects with other organizational functions (finance, marketing) for holistic success.
Systems Theory	Understanding how different parts interact is key to effective HR strategy development.
Interdependence	Recognizing that changes in one area can impact others is crucial for strategic planning.
Necessity of Feedback	Monitoring outcomes, adapting strategies based on feedback ensures continuous improvement.
Differentiation of Units	Acknowledging different departments may have unique needs is essential for effective HR strategy implementation.

Strategic Planning Analysis Frameworks:

Framework	Description
PESTLE Analysis	Analyzes Political, Economic, Social, Technological, Legal, and Environmental factors.

Framework	Description
SWOT Analysis	Examines Strengths, Weaknesses, Opportunities, Threats.
Industry Analysis	Considers competitors, trends, growth potential within the industry.
Location-Specific Analysis	Evaluates geographical factors impacting HR strategy (e.g., talent pool, labor laws).
Scenario Planning	Envisions possible future situations, develops contingency plans.
Growth-Share Matrix	Classifies businesses based on market share, growth potential to inform strategic HR decisions.
Real-Time Analysis	Utilizes data, analytics for continuous assessment of internal, external environment.
Blue Ocean Strategy	Focuses on creating new market space rather than competing in existing ones.

Strategic Planning Processes:

Phase	Description
Formulation	Defines organization's vision, mission, strategic goals.
Goal Setting	Establishes Specific, Measurable, Achievable, Relevant, Time-bound (SMART) goals aligned with strategy.
Implementation	Puts strategy into action through HR initiatives, programs, policies.
Evaluation	Regularly assesses effectiveness of HR strategy, makes adjustments as needed.

Understanding HR strategy and related concepts is crucial for success on the SHRM CP/SCP exam and in HR careers. Effective HR strategy optimizes human capital to achieve organizational goals and create stakeholder value.

Proficiency Indicators for All HR Professionals:

Indicator	Description
Uses the perspective of systems thinking to understand how the organization operates.	Utilizes systems thinking to comprehend organizational dynamics and interdependencies.
Informs business decisions with knowledge of the strategy and goals of HR and the organization.	Applies understanding of HR and organizational strategy to guide decision-making.
Develops and implements an individual action plan for executing HR's strategy and goals.	Creates and executes action plans aligned with HR strategy and objectives.
Uses benchmarks, industry metrics, and workforce trends to understand the organization's market position and competitive advantage.	Utilizes external benchmarks and internal metrics to assess market position and competitive advantage.
Informs HR leadership of new or overlooked opportunities to align HR's strategy with the organization's.	Identifies and communicates opportunities to align HR strategy with organizational objectives.
Provides HR leadership with timely and accurate information required for strategic decision-making.	Delivers relevant and precise information to HR leadership to support strategic decision-making.

Proficiency Indicators for Advanced HR Professionals:

Indicator	Description
Identifies the ways in which the HR function can support the organization's strategy and goals.	Recognizes opportunities for HR to contribute to organizational strategy and objectives.
Aligns strategic management and planning activities with organizational mission, vision, and values.	Ensures alignment between HR strategic activities and organizational mission, vision, and values.
Engages business leaders in strategic analysis and planning.	Involves business leaders in strategic discussions and planning processes.

Indicator	Description
Evaluates HR's critical activities in terms of value added, impact, and utility, using cost-benefit analysis, revenue, profit-and-loss estimates, and other leading or lagging indicators.	Assesses HR activities based on their contribution to organizational goals and outcomes, utilizing various analytical methods.
Provides HR-focused expertise to business leaders when formulating the organization's strategy and goals.	Offers HR expertise to business leaders during strategy formulation to ensure HR considerations are integrated.
Develops and implements HR strategy, vision, and goals that align with and support the organization's strategy and goals.	Creates and executes HR strategies that are in line with organizational objectives and contribute to their achievement.
Ensures that HR strategy creates and sustains the organization's competitive advantage.	Designs HR strategies to establish and maintain the organization's competitive edge in the market.

Domain 1: People Knowledge

Functional Area : (B) Talent Acquisition

Definition: Identifying, attracting, and building a qualified workforce to meet organizational needs.

Key Concepts:

Concept	Description
Employee Value Proposition (EVP) & Employment Branding	Create an appealing employer image highlighting company culture, growth opportunities, and purpose.
Job Analysis	Identify essential skills, knowledge, and abilities required for the job. Techniques: Task inventory, critical incidents, position analysis questionnaires.
Sourcing & Recruiting	Utilize various methods to find qualified candidates: External (job boards, social media) and Internal (job postings, employee referrals).
Selection Assessment	Evaluate candidate suitability through interviews, tests, assessments.
Employment Categories	Understand different types (full-time, part-time, contract, temporary, interns).
Job Offer & Negotiation	Consider salary, relocation, benefits, flexible work arrangements.

Concept	Description
Onboarding	Integrate new hires with orientation, buddy systems, personalization.
Metrics	Track key talent acquisition metrics (cost per hire, time to fill, candidate yield).
Technology	Utilize Applicant Tracking Systems (ATS), chatbots, AI resume screening.
Candidate Experience	Prioritize a streamlined application process, limited interview rounds, communication, respect for candidate time.

SHRM Proficiencies:

Proficiency	Description
Understand talent needs and diverse sourcing methods.	Recognize organizational talent requirements and utilize various sourcing channels effectively.
Leverage technology and promote EVP for effective recruiting.	Utilize technology and employer branding to attract and engage candidates.
Select candidates based on job requirements and organizational fit.	Evaluate candidates to ensure alignment with job roles and organizational culture.
Conduct legal pre-employment screening and onboarding.	Ensure compliance with legal requirements during pre-employment screening and onboarding processes.
Design job descriptions and advise managers on best practices.	Develop accurate job descriptions and provide guidance to managers on recruitment practices.

Advanced Proficiencies:

Advanced Proficiency	Description
Analyze staffing needs and develop sourcing strategies.	Assess organizational staffing requirements and devise effective sourcing strategies.

Advanced Proficiency	Description
Oversee talent acquisition processes and ensure effectiveness.	Manage end-to-end talent acquisition processes to optimize outcomes.
Design and implement successful onboarding programs.	Develop onboarding programs that facilitate new hire integration and engagement.

Domain 1: People Knowledge

Functional Area : (C) Employee Engagement & Retention

Definition: Building a thriving workforce and minimizing unwanted turnover.

Key Concepts:

Concept	Description
Organizational Culture	Develop and maintain a positive culture through learning, communication, strong values, and personalization. Impact: Improved performance, innovation, and risk-taking.
Workplace Flexibility	Offer programs like telecommuting, flexible schedules, and job sharing to enhance employee well-being.
Employee Engagement & Satisfaction	Utilize methods like surveys, focus groups, and stay interviews to assess employee sentiment. Job-attitude Theories: Engagement, satisfaction, commitment, involvement.
Job Design	Apply techniques like job enrichment, enlargement, rotation, and simplification to create more engaging work.
Employee Lifecycle	Understand the different phases (recruitment, integration, development, departure) to optimize HR strategies at each stage.
Retention Strategies	Implement best practices like realistic job previews, suggestion mechanisms, personalized onboarding, and effective performance management.
Performance Management	Utilize a system with dashboards, calibration, user training, and goal setting to provide frequent feedback and improve performance.

Concept	Description
Metrics	Track key metrics like quality of hire, voluntary turnover rate, turnover by location/level, and vacancy rate to monitor retention efforts.
Organizational Culture Types	Understand different cultures (authoritarian, mechanistic, participative, learning, high-performance) and their influence on employee engagement.
Recognition	Implement recognition programs like awards, point systems, peer-to-peer recognition, and personalized rewards to acknowledge achievements.
Employee Wellness	Offer programs for mental health, financial wellness, stress management, and work-life balance to support employee well-being.

SHRM Proficiencies:

Proficiency	Description
Conduct surveys, analyze data, and implement programs to improve employee experience, engagement, and culture.	Use data-driven approaches to enhance employee satisfaction and organizational culture.
Identify opportunities for job redesign to enhance motivation.	Modify job roles to increase employee engagement and motivation.
Monitor turnover metrics and coach supervisors on building positive work relationships.	Analyze turnover data and provide guidance to managers to improve employee retention.
Train stakeholders on performance management systems and employee performance expectations.	Educate employees and managers on performance management processes and expectations.
Measure the effectiveness of performance management systems.	Evaluate the impact of performance management systems on employee performance and organizational goals.

Advanced Proficiencies:

Advanced Proficiency	Description
Collaborate with leadership to create a positive employee experience and engaged workforce.	Work with senior management to foster a positive work environment and increase employee engagement.

Advanced Proficiency	Description
Implement best practices for employee retention in HR programs (career development, onboarding).	Incorporate retention strategies into HR initiatives to improve employee retention rates.
Design action plans based on employee engagement surveys.	Develop strategies to address issues identified in employee engagement surveys.
Oversee programs to improve employee engagement and satisfaction.	Lead initiatives to enhance employee engagement and satisfaction levels.
Monitor employee attitudes, turnover, and other engagement metrics.	Track key metrics to evaluate employee engagement and retention efforts.
Design and oversee performance management systems aligned with talent management needs.	Develop performance management systems that support talent development and organizational objectives.

Domain 1: People Knowledge

Functional Area : (D) Learning & Development

Definition: Equipping employees with the knowledge, skills, and abilities (KSAs) to achieve organizational goals.

Key Concepts:

Concept	Description
Needs Analysis	Identify skill gaps and training needs through methods like surveys, observations, and interviews. Types: Person, task, training, cost-benefit.
Learning & Development Program Design	Utilize models like ADDIE (Analyze, Design, Develop, Implement, Evaluate) to create effective training programs.
Adult Learning Theories	Understand how adults learn best. Example: 70-20-10 model: 70% experiential, 20% social interaction, 10% formal learning.

Concept	Description
Learning & Development Approaches	Utilize various methods to deliver training: Delivery Methods (e-learning, just-in-time, microlearning), Instructional Techniques (experiential learning, simulations), Content Formats (webinars, podcasts).
Developmental Assessments	Evaluate employee potential through methods like 360-degree assessments, skills assessments, and high-potential assessments.
Goal Setting	Establish effective goals using the SMART framework (Specific, Measurable, Achievable, Relevant, Time-bound) through Individual Development Plans (IDPs).
Career Development	Offer programs like career pathing, mentorship, cross-training, and job rotation to support career growth.
Knowledge Sharing	Facilitate knowledge transfer through methods like knowledge maps and knowledge cafes.
Leadership Development	Invest in leadership development programs and stretch assignments to develop future leaders.
Coaching & Mentoring	Implement formal and informal mentoring programs and coaching initiatives to foster a growth mindset.
Learning Technologies	Utilize Learning Management Systems (LMS), Artificial Intelligence (AI), Virtual Reality (VR), and chatbots to enhance learning experiences.

SHRM Proficiencies:

Proficiency	Description
Conduct needs assessments, develop training programs, and utilize resources to deliver effective learning.	Assess training needs, design programs, and deliver training effectively.
Foster knowledge sharing through internal social networks and IDP creation.	Facilitate knowledge sharing among employees and create Individual Development Plans.
Support knowledge transfer programs.	Promote programs to transfer knowledge effectively within the organization.

Advanced Proficiencies:

Advanced Proficiency	Description
Design strategies to identify critical skill gaps and develop relevant competencies.	Develop plans to address key skill gaps and build necessary competencies.
Monitor the effectiveness of leadership development programs.	Evaluate the impact of leadership development initiatives on organizational success.
Create long-term talent development strategies and knowledge retention plans.	Develop strategies to ensure the organization retains key knowledge and talent over time.

Domain 1: People Knowledge

Functional Area : (E) Total Rewards

Definition: Designing and implementing compensation and benefits programs to attract, retain, and motivate employees.

Key Concepts:

Concept	Description
Market Intelligence	Gather data on compensation and benefits trends through remuneration surveys and labor market analysis.
Data Analysis	Collect, interpret, and analyze compensation data using methods like comparable worth, benchmarking, etc.
Compensation Philosophies	Determine the approach to base pay (lead, lag, match, lead-lag) to position your company in the market.

Concept	Description
Compensation Plans	Develop plans for various employee groups considering special needs (e.g., salary, bonuses).
Leave Plans	Design leave programs including paid/unpaid leave, vacation, sick leave, parental leave, etc.
Retirement Planning	Offer retirement savings plans (pensions, savings plans) to support employee financial security.
Other Benefits	Provide a comprehensive benefits package including disability insurance, flexible work schedules, etc.
Other Compensation	Consider additional elements like deferred compensation, stock options, and tuition assistance.
Pay Practices	Manage pay practices effectively addressing issues like pay increases, pay equity, and pay transparency.
Payroll Accounting	Understand basic accounting principles for managing payroll.
Metrics & Benchmarks	Track key Total Rewards metrics to assess program effectiveness.

SHRM Proficiencies:

Proficiency	Description
Collect and interpret compensation and benefits data.	Analyze compensation data and trends to inform reward strategies.
Implement effective pay, benefit, and separation programs.	Design and administer compensation and benefits programs to meet organizational needs.
Comply with legal requirements governing compensation and benefits.	Ensure compliance with relevant laws and regulations related to compensation and benefits.
Understand different benefit approaches.	Recognize various approaches to providing employee benefits (e.g., government-mandated, voluntary).
Conduct job evaluations to determine compensation and benefits.	Evaluate job roles to establish fair and equitable compensation structures.

Advanced Proficiencies:

Advanced Proficiency	Description
Design and oversee Total Rewards strategies aligned with organizational goals.	Develop comprehensive Total Rewards strategies to support organizational objectives.
Design executive compensation plans linking performance to organizational success.	Develop executive compensation packages tied to performance metrics and organizational goals.
Ensure internal equity within compensation systems.	Maintain fairness and equity within compensation frameworks to avoid disparities.
Regularly evaluate and adjust the Total Rewards package.	Continuously review and update Total Rewards offerings to meet changing organizational needs and market trends.

Quiz Corner 10 - PEOPLE KNOWLEDGE DOMAIN

Stand-alone Knowledge-Based Questions:

1. What purpose is the PESTLE analysis framework used for?

a) Job evaluation
b) Strategic planning analysis
c) Competency assessment
d) Needs analysis

2. Which of the following is NOT a method for external recruitment?

a) Job boards
b) Employee referrals
c) Internal job postings
d) Social media recruitment

3. What does the "E" in the EVP (Employee Value Proposition) typically represent?

a) Salary and benefits
b) Opportunity for growth
c) Company culture
d) Work-life balance

4. What is the primary purpose of a stay interview?

a) To assess employee satisfaction
b) To develop an employee's skills
c) To onboard a new employee
d) To conduct performance management

5. A critical path analysis is used in project management to determine:

a) Team roles and responsibilities
b) The sequence of project tasks
c) The budget for the project
d) Communication strategies

Quiz Corner 10 - PEOPLE KNOWLEDGE DOMAIN

Stand-alone Knowledge-Based Questions:

6. What is the most common legal concern associated with background checks?

a) Not obtaining written consent from the candidate
b) Failing to provide a job offer after the check
c) Conducting the check too early in the hiring process
d) Disclosing inaccurate information in the report

7. What is the main benefit of using a competency model for recruitment?

a) To identify candidates with relevant experience
b) To assess a candidate's cultural fit
c) To ensure a diverse applicant pool
d) To evaluate a candidate's skills and knowledge

8. What is an example of an indirect cost associated with employee turnover?

a) Severance pay
b) Lost productivity
c) Signing bonus for a new hire
d) Training and development expenses for the departing employee

9. What is the key difference between a bonus and a merit increase?

a) Bonuses are typically awarded annually, while merit increases are given more frequently.
b) Bonuses are based on individual performance, while merit increases are based on cost of living.
c) Bonuses are a guaranteed part of an employee's compensation, while merit increases are not.
d) Bonuses are taxable, while merit increases are not.

10. Which of the following is NOT a vital component of an effective performance management system?

a) Goal setting
b) Regular feedback
c) Standardized performance appraisal forms
d) Opportunities for employee development

Quiz Corner 10 - PEOPLE KNOWLEDGE DOMAIN

Scenario-Based Situational Judgment Questions:

1. Scenario: A new manager has joined your company and seems to be struggling to build rapport with their team. They micromanage tasks and frequently criticize employees in public. How would you best address this situation?

A. Do nothing, as the manager is new and needs time to adjust.
B. Privately confront the manager and tell them to change their approach.
C. Schedule a private meeting with the manager to discuss their leadership style and its impact on the team. Offer coaching and resources on effective communication and team building.
D. Hold a team meeting and allow employees to voice their concerns directly to the manager.

2. During the interview process for a leadership role, a candidate makes a joke that could be considered offensive. While it seems unintentional, some interviewers feel uncomfortable. How do you proceed with the interview and selection process?

A. End the interview immediately and disqualify the candidate.
B. Address the joke directly with the candidate in a private setting, explain why it might be offensive, and gauge their understanding. Continue the interview while considering the candidate's overall tone and professionalism.
C. Ignore the comment and proceed with the interview as planned.
D. Ask the other interviewers to weigh in on whether to continue the interview.

3. An employee approaches you with concerns about a colleague who seems to be exhibiting signs of burnout. The employee is hesitant to speak to the colleague directly. What steps would you take?

A. Advise the employee to mind their own business and not get involved.
B. Thank the employee for coming forward and assure them of confidentiality. Offer to speak with the colleague privately to discuss workload or potential mental health concerns. Encourage the employee to document any specific incidents.
C. Encourage the employee to confront their colleague directly about their behavior.
D. Report the situation to the manager without the employee's knowledge.

4. Scenario: Two employees in the same department consistently disagree and have difficulty working together on projects. Their arguments are starting to affect team morale. How would you intervene?

A. Ignore the situation and hope it resolves itself.
B. Separate the two employees and assign them to different projects.
C. Facilitate a facilitated discussion between the two employees to identify the root cause of the conflict and explore potential solutions for improved communication and collaboration.
D. Issue a formal warning to both employees for their behavior.

5. Scenario: An employee asks for a flexible work arrangement due to childcare needs. However, their role requires them to be physically present in the office for a significant portion of the workday. How would you approach this request?

A. Deny the request as their role requires them to be in the office.
B. Explore alternative work arrangements like compressed workweeks or split schedules. If possible, consider some remote work options while maintaining core office hours for essential in-person tasks.
C. Offer to help the employee find alternative childcare arrangements.
D. Suggest the employee take a leave of absence until their childcare situation is resolved.

6. A customer complains that they were discriminated against based on age during the interview. How would you handle this situation?

- A. Dismiss the complaint as unfounded.
- B. Take the complaint seriously. Investigate the allegation thoroughly and follow company policies regarding discrimination. Ensure all hiring managers are trained in anti-discrimination practices.
- C. Offer the customer a discount on a product or service to apologize for the inconvenience.
- D. Delegate the investigation to a different HR representative.

7. A highly skilled employee informs you that they plan to leave the company for a better-paying opportunity. They are a valuable asset to the team. What would you do to try and retain them?

A. Accept their resignation without attempting to counteroffer.
B. Express appreciation for their contributions and inquire about their reasons for leaving. Explore options for salary negotiation, additional responsibilities, or professional development opportunities to address their concerns.
C. Offer them a glowing recommendation letter to help them find a new job.
D. Warn them about the risks of leaving a stable company for an uncertain opportunity.

8. During a performance review, employees become defensive and argue with their manager about their rating. How would you help facilitate a productive conversation?

A. Side with the employee and question the manager's judgment.
B. Tell the employee to accept the rating and move on.
C. Focus on specific examples and encourage the employee to provide their perspective. Actively listen and try to understand their viewpoint. Refocus on goals and areas for improvement and identify ways to support the employee's development.
D. Postpone the conversation and reschedule it for a later date.

9. Scenario: You notice that a senior manager's social media post contains offensive language that could damage the company's reputation. How would you address this issue?

- A. Publicly criticize the manager on social media.
- B. Ignore the post and hope it doesn't cause any problems.
- C. Discreetly approach the manager and explain the potential consequences of the post. Encourage them to remove the post or issue a clarifying statement. If necessary, involve higher management.
- D. Report the post to the social media platform and have it removed.

5. **Scenario**: The company is implementing a new HR technology platform, and some employees resist change. How would you encourage user adoption and address employee concerns?

A. Mandate all employees to use the new platform immediately.
B. Provide comprehensive training and resources on the new platform. Highlight the benefits for employees and address any specific concerns they may have. Offer ongoing support and answer questions throughout the implementation process.
C. Offer bonuses to the first employees to adopt the new platform.
D. Focus on the positive aspects of the new platform and avoid discussing any potential challenges.

Solution Quiz Corner 10 - PEOPLE KNOWLEDGE DOMAIN

Stand-alone Knowledge-Based Questions:

1. (b) Strategic planning analysis
2. (c) Internal job postings
3. (b) Opportunity for growth
4. (a) To assess employee satisfaction
5. (b) The sequence of project tasks
6. (a) Not obtaining written consent from the candidate
7. (d) To evaluate a candidate's skills and knowledge
8. (b) Lost productivity
9. (b) Bonuses are based on individual performance, while merit increases are based on cost of living.
10. (c) Standardized performance appraisal forms

Scenario-Based Situational Judgment Questions:

1. C. Schedule a private meeting with the manager to discuss their leadership style and its impact on the team. Offer coaching and resources on effective communication and team building. (**Explanation**: Choice C is the best approach. A direct but private conversation allows the HR professional to provide constructive feedback and suggest resources to help the manager improve their leadership skills.)
2. B. Address the joke directly with the candidate in a private setting, explain why it might be offensive, and gauge their understanding. Continue the interview while considering the candidate's overall tone and professionalism.(**Explanation**: Choice B allows the HR professional to address the situation directly while still giving the candidate a chance to explain themselves.)
3. B. Thank the employee for coming forward and assure them of confidentiality. Offer to speak with the colleague privately to discuss workload or potential mental health concerns. Encourage the employee to document any specific incidents. (**Explanation**: Choice B shows the HR professional taking a proactive and confidential approach to potentially help the struggling employee.)

Scenario-Based Situational Judgment Questions:

4. C. Facilitate a facilitated discussion between the two employees to identify the root cause of the conflict and explore potential solutions for improved communication and collaboration. (**Explanation**: Choice C demonstrates the HR professional's ability to address conflict constructively by facilitating a conversation where the employees can work towards resolving their differences.)

5. B. Explore alternative work arrangements like compressed workweeks or split schedules. Consider some remote work options while maintaining core office hours for essential in-person tasks if possible. (**Explanation**: Choice B showcases the HR professional's willingness to explore solutions that could accommodate the employee's needs while still meeting the requirements of the role.)

6. B. Take the complaint seriously. Investigate the allegation thoroughly and follow company policies regarding discrimination. Ensure all hiring managers are trained on anti-discrimination practices. (**Explanation**: Choice B is the most appropriate response. It demonstrates the HR professional's commitment to fair hiring practices and the need to handle discrimination complaints seriously.)

7. B. Express appreciation for their contributions and inquire about their specific reasons for leaving. Explore options for salary negotiation, additional responsibilities, or professional development opportunities to address their concerns. (**Explanation**: Choice B shows the HR professional taking steps to understand the employee's motivations and potentially address their concerns to retain them.)

8. C. Focus on specific examples and encourage the employee to provide their perspective. Actively listen and try to understand their viewpoint. Refocus on goals and areas for improvement and identify ways to support the employee's development. (**Explanation**: Choice C demonstrates active listening and facilitation skills to help navigate a potentially difficult conversation.)

9. C. Discreetly approach the manager and explain the potential consequences of the post. Encourage them to remove the post or issue a clarifying statement. If necessary, involve higher management. (**Explanation**: Choice C prioritizes a private and professional approach to address the issue with the manager while taking steps to mitigate potential reputational damage..)

10. B. Provide comprehensive training and resources on the new platform. Highlight the benefits for employees and address any specific concerns they may have. Offer ongoing support and answer questions throughout the implementation process. (**Explanation**:Choice B outlines a clear communication and training strategy to encourage user adoption and address employee concerns about the new platform.)

7. Domain 2: Organizational Knowledge

Technical Competency-Domain 2: Organizational Knowledge

The HR Expertise competency is one technical competency which outlines **14 functional areas grouped into three domains.**

Domain 1: People Knowledge	Domain 2: Organizational Knowledge	Domain 3: Workplace Knowledge
HR Strategy	**Structure of the HR Function**	Managing a Global Workforce
Talent Acquisition	**Organizational Effectiveness and Development**	Risk Management
Employee Engagement and Retention	**Workforce Management**	Corporate Social Responsibility
Learning and Development	**Employee Labor and Relations**	US Employment Law and Regulations
Total Rewards	**Technology Management**	

Learning Objectives:

- Understand critical HR knowledge relating to the organization.
- Identify functional areas within the Organization's Knowledge Domain.
- Apply HR practices to achieve organizational goals.

Functional Areas

Functional Area	Description
Structure of the HR Function	- Designing an HR department aligned with organizational strategy (centralized, decentralized, etc.). - Staffing the HR department with skilled professionals. - Establishing clear reporting structures and lines of authority

Functional Area	Description
Organizational Effectiveness & Development	• Performance management practices to evaluate and improve organizational performance. • Strategies for organizational change management. • Developing a culture of continuous improvement.
Workforce Management	• Workforce planning to ensure the right talent is available at the right time. • Job analysis and design to define work requirements and skills needed. • Staffing strategies for recruitment, selection, onboarding, and retention.
Employee & Labor Relations	• Promoting positive employee relations through communication and engagement. • Managing conflict resolution and grievance procedures. • Understanding and complying with labor laws and regulations.
Technology Management	• Selecting and implementing HR technology solutions. • Utilizing technology to improve HR processes and data management. • Ensuring data security and privacy compliance.

Key Points:

- HR professionals align HR practices with organizational strategy.
- Effective HR practices contribute to organizational effectiveness and development.
- Talent and workforce management are crucial for achieving organizational goals.
- Positive employee relations foster a healthy and productive work environment.
- Technology enhances HR efficiency and effectiveness.

Examples:

- Implementing a performance management system tied to organizational goals.
- Developing a training program to address identified skill gaps through job analysis.
- Using an applicant tracking system to streamline recruitment.
- Negotiating a collective bargaining agreement with a union.
- Utilizing HR analytics to inform decision-making.

Domain 2: ORGANIZATION KNOWLEDGE DOMAIN

Functional Area : (A) Structure of the HR Function
Structure

Definition: This Functional; Area delves into the Structure of the HR Function, exploring its components and their role in delivering essential HR services and driving organizational effectiveness.

Key Concepts:

Concept	Description
HR Service Models	Define how HR services are delivered. Examples include Centralized, Decentralized, and Global Resources models.
HR Structural Models	Define the internal organization of the HR department. Examples include Center of Excellence (COE), Shared Services, Business Partners, and Matrix models.
Elements of the HR Function	Core HR activities such as Recruiting & Talent Management, Compensation & Benefits, Training & Development, Employee Relations, and HR Compliance.
HR Staff Roles & Responsibilities	Roles within the HR department, including HR Generalists, Specialists, and Business Partners.
Outsourcing HR Functions	Outsourcing specific HR activities to external vendors, such as Recruiting, Benefits Administration, and Payroll.
HR Function Metrics	Measurement of HR effectiveness through metrics like HR Staff per Full-Time Employee, Customer Satisfaction, Key Performance Indicators (KPIs), and Balanced Scorecard.

SHRM Proficiency Indicators:

Indicator	Description
All HR Professionals	Adapt to the organization's HR service model. Seek stakeholder feedback. Act as an HR point-of-contact. Collaborate with leadership. Integrate outsourced/automated HR functions. Analyze HR KPIs. Collaborate with other departments.
Advanced HR Professionals	Design and implement the HR service model. Implement changes based on stakeholder feedback. Ensure alignment across all HR elements. Identify opportunities for outsourcing or automation. Design and oversee HR metrics programs.

Domain 2: ORGANIZATION KNOWLEDGE DOMAIN

Functional Area : (B) Organizational Effectiveness & Development

Structure

Definition: This Functional Area delves into Organizational Effectiveness & Development (OE&D), a crucial domain for HR professionals focusing on the organization's overall health and continuous improvement.

Key Concepts:

Concept	Description
Group Dynamics	Understanding how groups function, including intergroup & intragroup dynamics, formation, identity, cohesion, structure, and influence.
Conflict Management	Recognizing and resolving disagreements within groups effectively.
Tuckman's Stages of Group Development	Forming, Storming, Norming, and Performing stages in group dynamics.

Concept	Description
Organizational Design Structures	Different structures like Customer-Centric, Functional, Geographic, Matrix, and Program/Product-Based.
Organizational Analysis	Evaluation of organizational health through performance analysis and frameworks like McKinsey 7S Framework.

SHRM Proficiency Indicators:

Indicator	Description
All HR Professionals	Ensure HR documents reflect actual work activities. Support initiatives to improve HR systems and processes. Identify areas needing change. Collect and analyze data on organizational performance.
Advanced HR Professionals	Align HR strategy with the organization's mission and vision. Monitor results against performance goals. Establish measurable goals. Consult on, design, and plan organizational structures. Assess organizational needs. Design and oversee change initiatives. Ensure HR initiatives demonstrate measurable value.

HR plays a pivotal role in OE&D. Understanding group dynamics, organizational design, and analyzing organizational health equips HR professionals to drive continuous improvement and long-term success.

Domain 2: ORGANIZATION KNOWLEDGE DOMAIN

Functional Area : (C) Workforce Management

Definition: Workforce Management (WFM) is essential for HR professionals to ensure the organization has the right talent to achieve its goals. This chapter explores vital WFM practices for managing talent needs and addressing critical skill gaps effectively.

Key Concepts:

Concept	Description
Workforce Planning	Proactive strategies to anticipate future talent needs, including forecasting, talent development, and attrition analysis.
Upskilling & Reskilling Employees	Equipping employees with new or advanced skills to meet evolving demands through training and development initiatives.
Job Redesign	Modifying job roles to align with changing organizational needs and technological advancements.
Identifying High-Potential & High-Performance Employees	Recognizing talent for future leadership or critical roles within the organization.
Knowledge Management	Strategies for capturing, sharing, and applying organizational knowledge to enhance productivity and innovation.
Succession Planning	Ensuring a pipeline of qualified talent for future leadership roles through mentorship and talent development programs.
Restructuring & Downsizing	Strategies for workforce adjustments during mergers, acquisitions, or economic changes, including layoffs and furloughs.

SHRM Proficiency Indicators:

Indicator	Description
All HR Professionals	Assess talent needs and skill gaps, develop workforce plans, support succession planning, and provide learning opportunities.
Advanced HR Professionals	Evaluate workforce capabilities, collaborate on leadership development, and lead restructuring efforts as needed.

Workforce Management is vital for organizational success. By implementing effective strategies for talent acquisition, development, and restructuring, HR professionals can ensure the organization has the right talent to thrive in a dynamic business environment.

Domain 2: ORGANIZATION KNOWLEDGE DOMAIN

Functional Area : (D) Employee & Labor Relations

Definition: This Functional Area of Employee & Labor Relations (E&LR) is crucial for managing interactions between the organization and its employees regarding terms and conditions of employment. This chapter explores key concepts to promote a positive work environment and effectively handle disputes.

Key Concepts:

Concept	Description
International Labour Organization (ILO) Standards	Fundamental worker rights established by the ILO, including labor rights, fair wages, and standard workday.
Compliance & Ethics Programs	Programs designed to ensure adherence to regulations and ethical standards, including policy development and performance measurement.
Alternative Dispute Resolution (ADR)	Methods for resolving workplace conflicts outside of court, such as mediation and arbitration.
Retaliation Prevention	Strategies to prevent retaliation against employees who raise concerns, including open-door policies and whistleblower protection.
Workplace Investigations	Thorough and objective investigations into employee misconduct, ensuring consistency and fairness.
Progressive Discipline	A structured approach to disciplinary action, progressing from counseling to termination if necessary.
Grievance & Complaint Resolution	Formal procedures for addressing employee grievances, including investigation and appeal processes.
Strikes, Lockouts, & Boycotts	Understanding causes and strategies for addressing labor disputes, such as strike response plans.

SHRM Proficiency Indicators:

Indicator	Description
All HR Professionals	Develop policies promoting positive relations, advise on employment terms, guide managers on disciplinary actions, and manage grievance processes.
Advanced HR Professionals	Develop labor relations strategies, educate employees on policy changes, coach managers, and lead negotiations with employee representatives.

Effective E&LR practices foster a positive work environment, minimize legal risks, and ensure fair treatment of all employees. By understanding key legal and ethical considerations, HR professionals can effectively manage labor relations and contribute to organizational success.

Domain 2: ORGANIZATION KNOWLEDGE DOMAIN

Functional Area : (E) Technology Management

Definition: Technology Management is essential for HR professionals to leverage technology effectively in the workplace. This chapter explores HR technology solutions, data management practices, and strategies for governing technology use.

Key Concepts:

- HR Technology & Software: Examples include Applicant Tracking Systems (ATS), HR Information Systems (HRIS), Learning Management Systems (LMS), and Artificial Intelligence (AI).
- Data & Information Management: Ensuring data security, integrity, and compliance with regulations through strategies like data backups and cybersecurity measures.
- Electronic Self-Service (ESS): Empowering employees and managers to manage HR tasks independently through technology, such as benefits enrollment and scheduling.
- Technology Use Standards & Policies: Establish clear workplace technology use guidelines, including BYOD policies and social media management.

SHRM Proficiency Indicators:

- **All HR Professionals**: Implement HR technology solutions, safeguard data confidentiality, and guide stakeholders on proper technology use.
- **Advanced HR Professionals:** Evaluate and implement technology aligned with strategic goals, select optimal vendors, and collaborate with business leaders on technology initiatives.

Remember:

Understanding and leveraging technology effectively can streamline HR processes, improve decision-making, and empower HR professionals and employees. It's crucial for HR professionals to stay updated on the latest technology trends and best practices.

Quiz Corner 11 - ORGANIZATION KNOWLEDGE DOMAIN

Stand-alone Knowledge-Based Questions:

1. Which of the following is NOT an element of the HR function?

a) Recruiting
b) Training and development
c) Marketing
d) Compensation and benefits

2. A generalist HR professional is most likely responsible for:

a) Designing a new talent management program.
b) Overseeing the implementation of a new HR information system.
c) Handling all HR tasks for a small department.
d) Providing legal advice on employment matters.

3. What is the primary purpose of HR metrics?

a) To track employee satisfaction.
b) To measure the effectiveness of HR programs.
c) To monitor compliance with labor laws.
d) To assess the financial performance of the organization.

4. What is an example of a centralized HR service delivery model?

a) HR professionals are embedded within business units.
b) A dedicated HR team handles all HR functions for the organization.
c) HR tasks are outsourced to a third-party provider.
d) HR responsibilities are shared among different departments.

5. Which of the following is NOT a key concept in organizational design structures?

a) Customer focus
b) Geographic location
c) Job titles
d) Functional specialization

Quiz Corner 11 - ORGANIZATION KNOWLEDGE DOMAIN

Stand-alone Knowledge-Based Questions:

6. What is the term for identifying and addressing gaps between an organization's current and future workforce needs?

a) Performance appraisal
b) Workforce planning
c) Succession planning
d) Outplacement

7. Which of the following is an example of a non-traditional staffing method?

a) On-campus recruiting
b) Internal job posting
c) Temporary workers
d) Management training programs

8. What is the primary objective of an organization's code of conduct?

a) To outline employee benefits and compensation plans.
b) To define acceptable workplace behaviors and ethical standards.
c) To document performance management procedures.
d) To specify disciplinary actions for misconduct.

9. What is the key difference between mediation and arbitration in workplace conflict resolution?

a) Mediation is non-binding, while arbitration is binding.
b) Mediation involves a neutral third party facilitating discussion, while arbitration involves a third party making a final decision.
c) Mediation is used for minor issues, while arbitration is for major issues.
d) Mediation requires legal representation, while arbitration does not.

10. What is the primary focus of competency-based talent management?

a) Identifying and developing leadership skills.
b) Matching employee skills and experience to specific job requirements.
c) Promoting employee well-being and engagement.
d) Providing opportunities for career advancement.

Quiz Corner 11 - ORGANIZATION KNOWLEDGE DOMAIN

Scenario-Based Situational Judgment Questions:

1. You are the HR manager for a large retail company. A new policy requiring employees to wear fitness trackers has sparked controversy. Some employees feel the policy is an invasion of privacy, while others appreciate the potential health benefits. How should you address this situation?

a) Implement the policy as planned and offer a one-time opt-out option for religious reasons.
b) Hold company-wide meetings to explain the policy benefits and address privacy concerns.
c) Conduct a confidential employee survey to gauge opinions and concerns before implementing the policy.
d) Withdraw the policy entirely and focus on promoting healthy habits through existing wellness programs.

2. You are the HR business partner for the marketing department. A high-performing marketing manager has recently developed a hostile work environment for their team members. Several employees have approached you with complaints about the manager's behavior. What is the best course of action?

a) Conduct an informal conversation with the manager to address the complaints and encourage a change in behavior.
b) Immediately launch a formal investigation into the allegations of a hostile work environment.
c) Document the employee complaints and advise them to confront the manager directly about their behavior.
d) Recommend the manager attend leadership training to improve communication and interpersonal skills.

3. You are the HR representative for a manufacturing plant. Two employees on the same team have been in a heated argument for weeks, impacting team productivity. How can you best resolve this conflict?

a) Separate the two employees and assign them to different teams.
b) Schedule a private mediation session with both employees to facilitate communication and find a resolution.
c) Issue written warnings to both employees for disruptive behavior.
d) Advise the team leader to handle the situation and encourage them to work it out amongst themselves.

4. You are the HR generalist for a growing tech startup. Several employees have expressed concerns about feeling overwhelmed and stressed due to a heavy workload and tight deadlines. What steps can you take to address this issue?

a) Encourage employees to work longer hours to meet deadlines.
b) Implement a company-wide mental health awareness campaign.
c) Analyze workload distribution and consider hiring additional staff or delegating tasks.
d) Offer free access to stress-reduction apps and encourage employees to take more breaks.

5. You are the HR director for a financial services company. A senior manager has been accused of sexual harassment by a junior employee. How should you handle this situation?

a) Advise the junior employee to handle the situation directly with the manager.
b) Investigate the allegation internally and take appropriate disciplinary action if necessary.
c) Offer the junior employee a transfer to a different department.
d) Consult with legal counsel immediately and launch a thorough investigation.

6. You work in HR for a healthcare organization. A nurse has requested a flexible work arrangement due to childcare needs. The manager is hesitant due to potential staffing challenges. How can you help facilitate a solution?

a) Deny the request for a flexible work arrangement due to the manager's concerns.
b) Work with the manager to explore alternative staffing options, such as job sharing or temporary staffing, to address their concerns.
c) Advise the nurse to find alternative childcare arrangements to meet the manager's scheduling needs. d) Approve the flexible work arrangement immediately without considering the manager's input.

7. You are the HR business partner for a construction company. A group of employees approaches you with concerns about safety protocols on a new project site. They believe the current protocols are inadequate and could lead to accidents. What should you do?

a) Advise the employees to follow the existing protocols and report any safety hazards to their supervisor.
b) Thank the employees for their feedback and conduct a follow-up inspection of the project site with a safety specialist.
c) Schedule a meeting with the project manager to discuss the employees' concerns and ensure all safety protocols are being followed.
d) Organize a safety training session for all employees working on the project site.

8. You are the HR manager for a hospitality company. A customer has filed a formal complaint against a hotel employee for rude and unprofessional behavior. How should you handle this situation?

a) Discount customers' complaints and offer them a complimentary stay on their next visit.
b) Review the complaint details with the employee and provide coaching on customer service skills.
c) Launch a formal investigation into the employee's conduct and take appropriate disciplinary action if necessary.
d) Offer the customer a full refund for their stay and apologize for the inconvenience.

9. You are the HR generalist for a non-profit organization. A long-term employee has announced their retirement. The employee possesses a wealth of institutional knowledge and is interested in mentoring new hires. How can you leverage this opportunity?

a) Assign the retiring employee a formal mentoring role with a set schedule and compensation.
b) Develop a volunteer program where the retiring employee can share their knowledge ad-hoc.
c) Organize knowledge-transfer sessions where the retiring employee can train new hires on specific skills and processes.
d) Document the retiring employee's knowledge and expertise to create training materials for future use.

10. You are the HR director for a manufacturing company experiencing a downturn in business. Management has decided to lay off a significant number of employees. How can you ensure a fair and transparent layoff process?

a) Select employees for layoff based on their performance reviews.
b) Offer severance packages to all employees who are laid off.
c) Develop clear layoff selection criteria and communicate them openly to all employees.
d) Provide outplacement services to help laid-off employees find new jobs.

Solution Quiz Corner 11 - ORGANIZATION KNOWLEDGE DOMAIN

Stand-alone Knowledge-Based Questions:

1. (c) Marketing is not a core element of the HR function.
2. (c) Generalists handle various HR tasks for a specific department or unit.
3. (b) HR metrics help assess the effectiveness of HR programs in achieving organizational goals.
4. (b) A centralized model concentrates HR functions in a dedicated team.
5. (c) Job titles are not a defining characteristic of organizational design structures.
6. (b) Workforce planning
7. (c) Temporary workers
8. (b) To define acceptable workplace behaviors and ethical standards.
9. (b) Mediation involves a neutral third party facilitating discussion, while arbitration involves a third party making a final decision.
10. (b) Matching employee skills and experience to specific job requirements.

Scenario-Based Situational Judgment Questions:

1. **Answer:** (c) Conduct a confidential employee survey to gauge opinions and concerns before implementing the policy. (**Explanation**: This approach lets you gather data on employee sentiment and concerns before enforcing a potentially divisive policy. The feedback can be used to refine the policy, address privacy issues, or potentially develop alternative wellness initiatives.)
2. **Answer:** (b) Immediately launch a formal investigation into the allegations of a hostile work environment. **Explanation**: A hostile work environment can have serious legal implications. A formal investigation ensures a fair and objective process to gather evidence, protect employees, and determine appropriate disciplinary action.
3. **Answer:** (b) Schedule a private mediation session with both employees to facilitate communication and find a resolution. **Explanation**: Mediation provides a safe space for open communication. A neutral third party can help identify the root cause of the conflict and work towards a solution that satisfies both parties.
4. **Answer:** (c) Analyze workload distribution and consider hiring additional staff or delegating tasks. **Explanation**: While mental health resources are valuable, the root cause appears to be workload. Addressing workload through additional staffing or task delegation will alleviate stress and improve employee well-being.
5. **Answer**: (d) Consult with legal counsel immediately and launch a thorough investigation. **Explanation**: Sexual harassment allegations are serious and require immediate attention. Consulting legal counsel ensures a fair and compliant investigation to protect the rights of both parties.
6. **Answer**: b) Work with the manager to address their concerns and explore alternative staffing options, such as job sharing or temporary staffing. **Explanation:** This approach acknowledges the manager's staffing concerns while seeking creative solutions to accommodate the nurse's childcare needs. Exploring alternative staffing options demonstrates flexibility and a commitment to supporting both the employee and the department's operational needs.

Scenario-Based Situational Judgment Questions:

7. **Answer**: (b) Thank the employees for their feedback and conduct a follow-up inspection of the project site with a safety specialist.
Explanation: Employee concerns about safety should be taken seriously. A follow-up inspection with a safety specialist allows for an objective assessment of the protocols and ensures any potential hazards are addressed promptly.

8. **Answer**: (c) Launch a formal investigation into the employee's conduct and take appropriate disciplinary action if necessary.
Explanation: Customer complaints need to be addressed to maintain a positive brand image and ensure guest satisfaction. A formal investigation allows for due process while protecting both the customer and the employee.

9. **Answer**: (d) Document the retiring employee's knowledge and expertise to create training materials for future use.
Explanation: Formalizing a mentoring role could be time-consuming for the retiree. By documenting their knowledge, the organization can preserve valuable institutional memory in a format that is easily accessible to future employees.

10. **Answer**: (c) Develop clear layoff selection criteria and communicate them openly to all employees.
Explanation: Transparency and fairness are crucial during layoffs. Clearly defined criteria for layoff selection minimizes bias and allows employees to understand the process. While severance packages and outplacement services are beneficial, open communication is essential for maintaining trust during a difficult time.

8. Domain 3: Workplace Knowledge Domain

Technical Competency-Domain 3: Workplace Knowledge

The HR Expertise competency is one technical competency which outlines **14 functional areas grouped into three domains.**

Domain 1: People Knowledge	Domain 2: Organizational Knowledge	Domain 3: Workplace Knowledge
HR Strategy	Structure of the HR Function	**Managing a Global Workforce**
Talent Acquisition	Organizational Effectiveness and Development	**Risk Management**
Employee Engagement and Retention	Workforce Management	**Corporate Social Responsibility**
Learning and Development	Employee Labor and Relations	**US Employment Law and Regulations**
Total Rewards	Technology Management	

Learning Objectives:

This chapter equips you with essential HR knowledge crucial for the SHRM CP/SCP exams. By mastering these concepts, you'll excel in:

Functional Areas

Managing a Global Workforce

- Recruiting, onboarding, and training diverse international talent.
- Cultivating cultural competency for effective global talent management.
- Crafting compensation and benefits strategies for international employees.
- Navigating labor relations and compliance with varied employment laws worldwide.

Risk Management

- Identifying and assessing workplace risks: safety hazards, legal issues, etc.
- Implementing risk mitigation strategies and policies.
- Ensuring a safe work environment and crisis management readiness.

Corporate Social Responsibility (CSR)

- Embracing CSR principles: environmental sustainability, social justice, ethics.
- Designing initiatives benefiting employees, community, and environment.
- Measuring and reporting CSR progress for transparency and accountability.

U.S. Employment Law & Regulations

- Understanding federal laws (e.g., FLSA, ADA, FMLA) and their HR implications.
- Navigating state and local regulations for comprehensive compliance.
- Staying abreast of legal changes to ensure adherence and mitigate risks.

Examples and Case Studies

- **Global Workforce Management**: Analyze a case study on successful international expansion strategies.
- **Risk Management Practices**: Explore real-world examples showcasing effective risk mitigation in various workplace contexts.
- **CSR Impact Assessment**: Evaluate a CSR program's effect on company reputation and employee engagement.
- **Legal Scenario Analysis**: Apply knowledge of U.S. employment law to resolve hypothetical HR dilemmas.

Definitions and Examples

Concept	Definition	Example
Cultural Competency	Ability to interact effectively with people of different cultures.	Example: Providing cross-cultural training for managers overseeing global teams.

Concept	Definition	Example
Crisis Management Planning	Preparation and response procedures to handle emergencies or unexpected events.	Example: Conducting regular drills to ensure employees know how to evacuate during a fire.
Corporate Social Responsibility (CSR)	Business approach contributing to sustainable development by delivering economic, social, and environmental benefits.	Example: Implementing volunteer programs for employees to engage with local communities.
Fair Labor Standards Act (FLSA)	Federal law governing minimum wage, overtime pay, recordkeeping, and child labor standards.	Example: Ensuring non-exempt employees receive overtime pay for hours worked beyond 40 in a workweek.
Family and Medical Leave Act (FMLA)	Federal law providing eligible employees unpaid, job-protected leave for specified family and medical reasons.	Example: Granting an employee 12 weeks of FMLA leave to care for a newborn child or ailing family member.
Americans with Disabilities Act (ADA)	Federal law prohibiting discrimination against individuals with disabilities in all areas of public life.	Example: Providing reasonable accommodations, such as wheelchair ramps or flexible work schedules, for employees with disabilities.
Environmental Sustainability	Actions and strategies aimed at preserving natural resources and reducing ecological footprint.	Example: Implementing energy-efficient practices, like switching to LED lighting or reducing paper usage in the office.
Social Justice	Pursuit of fairness and equality in society, addressing systemic issues and promoting equitable opportunities.	Example: Advocating for diversity and inclusion initiatives to ensure fair representation and opportunities for all employees.
Ethical Business Practices	Conducting business in accordance with moral principles, integrity, and honesty.	Example: Establishing a whistleblower hotline to report unethical behavior without fear of retaliation.

Domain 2: Workplace Knowledge Domain

Functional Area : (A) Managing a Global Workforce

Definition:

"Managing a Global Workforce" encompasses overseeing diverse talent across international boundaries to ensure organizational success. It involves navigating immigration, mobility, and cultural nuances while optimizing talent deployment and compliance with legal and strategic objectives.

Key Concepts

HR Structures for Global Work	Examples
Immigration and mobility specialists	HR professionals adept in visa processes and relocation logistics.
Geographic centers of excellence	Centralizing expertise strategically across global locations.
Global job classifications	Standard job descriptions tailored to local contexts.
International business travel policies	Guidelines covering expense management, safety, and cultural considerations during travel.

Immigration and Mobility

Key Aspects	Examples
Relevant laws	Understanding visa types, work permits, and tax implications.
Visa processes and requirements	Navigating procedures for obtaining visas in different countries.
Sponsorship expenses	Assessing financial obligations for sponsoring foreign workers.

Immigration and Mobility

Key Practices	Examples
Performance expectations and evaluations	Setting clear goals and conducting culturally sensitive reviews.
Health and safety	Providing medical insurance, security briefings, and evacuation plans.

Key Practices	Examples
Compensation adjustments	Adapting salaries for cost of living and tax disparities.
Socialization	Facilitating integration into the new work environment and local community.
Assessing employee and family readiness	Evaluating willingness and ability to adapt to new environments.
Training on culture and resources	Guiding on cultural norms, language, and available support systems.
Language training	Investing in language skills for effective communication.
Education travel grants	Offering financial assistance for relocating employees' children's education.
Rental subsidies	Providing housing support considering local housing costs.
Transition plans	Developing roadmaps for smooth relocation and onboarding.
Repatriation	Planning successful return to home country post-assignment.

Methods for Moving Work

Key Methods	Examples
Offshoring	Transferring jobs abroad for cost savings.
Onshoring	Bringing jobs back to home country due to automation or strategic reasons.
Nearshoring	Moving jobs to geographically closer countries for improved collaboration.
Remote teams	Utilizing technology for employees to work from anywhere.

Proficiency Indicators

For All HR Professionals:

- Stay updated on global PESTLE factors and their workforce implications.
- Manage HR activities for a global, mobile workforce.

- Balance standardization of HR practices with local legal and cultural needs.
- Oversee immigration and mobility programs with compliance.
- Manage day-to-day activities related to international assignments.

For Advanced HR Professionals:

- Analyze and influence global PESTLE factors to support organizational strategies.
- Develop comprehensive strategies for managing global workforces.
- Collaborate with business leaders to integrate global competencies.
- Establish and manage immigration and mobility programs for compliance.
- Identify opportunities to optimize costs and talent by moving work across borders.
- Design international assignment programs aligned with organizational goals.

Domain 2: Workplace Knowledge Domain

Functional Area : (B) Risk Management

Definition:

"Risk Management" involves systematically identifying, assessing, and mitigating potential threats to an organization's objectives. It encompasses strategies to minimize adverse impacts and optimize opportunities for organizational success. It proactively addresses hazards, uncertainties, and vulnerabilities to safeguard assets, reputation, and stakeholder interests.

Key Concepts

Concept	Description
Enterprise Risk Management (ERM)	Structured approach to identify, assess, prioritize, and control organizational threats, incorporating risk understanding, analysis, and treatment.

Concept	Description
Risk Assessment Techniques	Qualitative (severity and likelihood evaluation) and Quantitative (assigning numerical values to probability and impact).
Risk Sources and Types	Internal (e.g., project failures) and External (e.g., economic downturns), categorized into Hazard, Financial, Operational, and Strategic risks.
Compliance and Investigations	Auditing and Investigation Techniques, Quality Assurance, and Business Continuity Planning.
Emergency and Disaster Preparedness	Planning for various emergencies/disasters, including communication, evacuation, and training.
Safety and Security	Addressing concerns like workplace violence, theft, fraud, cyber threats, and ensuring workplace safety and health.
Drug-Free Workplace	Establishing policies, conducting testing, and offering resources for substance abuse treatment.

Proficiency Indicators

Proficiency Indicators	Description
For All HR Professionals:	
Monitor PESTLE factors	Stay updated on factors influencing organizational risk.
Implement HR programs	Develop and implement programs mitigating workplace risks.
Assist in crisis management	Contribute to crisis management, contingency, and business continuity plans.
Communicate risk information	Effectively communicate risk information to all employees.
Conduct investigations	Conduct investigations related to legal compliance and workplace safety/health.
Audit risk management plans	Ensure accurate reporting and audit risk management plans.
Consider risk levels	Consider risk levels when evaluating business proposals.

Proficiency Indicators

Proficiency Indicators	Description
For Advanced HR Professionals:	
Develop formal processes	Develop formal processes for identifying and monitoring risks.
Analyze labor market	Analyze labor market, industry, and global trends' impact on risk.
Advise leadership	Advise leadership on threats and develop comprehensive risk management strategies.
Oversee crisis management	Oversee crisis management for HR and the organization.
Communicate critical risk information	Communicate critical risk information to senior management and stakeholders.
Regularly audit risk mitigation	Regularly audit and improve risk mitigation strategies.
Lead workplace safety investigations	Lead workplace safety investigations and address violence and retaliation.
Evaluate risks	Evaluate risks associated with potential strategic opportunities.

Domain 2: Workplace Knowledge Domain

Functional Area : (C) Corporate Social Responsibility

Definition:

CSR is an organization's initiative to operate ethically and contribute positively to society, focusing on economic development, employee well-being, and community engagement.

HR's Role in CSR

Activity	Description	Example
Sustainability Practices	Embedding social responsibility throughout HR functions.	Diversity & Inclusion programs, fair labor practices.

Implementing a CSR Strategy

Step	Description
Develop Business Case	Highlight benefits of CSR (e.g., brand reputation, employee engagement).
Gain Leadership Approval	Secure buy-in from senior management.
Select Recipients	Choose initiatives aligned with organizational values.
Identify Performance Indicators	Define metrics to track CSR impact (e.g., volunteer hours).
Organize & Recruit Participants	Engage employees in CSR activities.

Community Engagement

Approach	Description	Example
Board Representation	HR professionals serving on community boards.	Local education board participation.
Joint Projects	Collaborating with community organizations.	Building a community park with a local NGO.
Employee Volunteerism	Encouraging employees to volunteer their time.	Beach clean-up day organized by HR department.

SHRM Proficiency Indicators

For All HR Professionals:

- Be a role model for ethical conduct and community engagement.
- Promote HR involvement in CSR activities aligned with organizational strategy.
- Identify opportunities for environmentally and socially responsible practices.
- Educate staff on the societal impact of business decisions and CSR's role in community improvement.
- Maintain transparency in HR programs and policies.
- Coach managers on fostering transparency in organizational practices.

For Advanced HR Professionals:

- Develop a CSR strategy reflecting the organization's mission and values.
- Integrate CSR objectives across the organization with business leaders.
- Develop transparency and self-governance practices with leadership.
- Partner with leaders to encourage responsible business decisions.
- Align CSR activities with workforce and community engagement.
- Use metrics to demonstrate the value proposition of CSR programs (e.g., employee satisfaction, competitive advantage).

Domain 2: Workplace Knowledge Domain

Functional Area : (D) U.S. Employment Law & Regulations

Definition:

Understanding U.S. Employment Law & Regulations is paramount for HR professionals, encompassing diverse legal principles governing workplace practices and employee rights.

Key Concepts

Employment and Authorization to Work

- Focus: Verifying an employee's legal right to work in the U.S.
- Key Laws: Immigration Reform and Control Act (IRCA) of 1986.
- Other Considerations: Employment at Will, Background Checks.

Compensation

- Focus: Ensuring fair and legal pay practices.
- Key Laws: Fair Labor Standards Act (FLSA), Equal Pay Act.
- Other Considerations: Davis-Bacon and Walsh-Healey Acts, Employee Retirement Income Security Act (ERISA).

Employee Relations

- Focus: Maintaining a legal framework for unions and labor relations.
- Key Laws: National Labor Relations Act (NLRA), Labor Management Relations Act (LMRA).
- Other Considerations: Worker Adjustment and Retraining Notification Act (WARN).

Job Safety and Health

- Focus: Providing a safe and healthy work environment.
- Key Laws: Occupational Safety and Health Act (OSHA), Americans with Disabilities Act (ADA).
- Other Considerations: Drug-Free Workplace Act, Health Insurance Portability and Accountability Act (HIPAA).

Equal Employment Opportunity (EEO)

- Focus: Preventing discrimination in employment decisions.
- Key Laws are the Civil Rights Act of 1964, the Age Discrimination in Employment Act (ADEA), and the Americans with Disabilities Act (ADA).
- Other Considerations: Equal Employment Opportunity Act (EEOC).

Leave and Benefits

- Focus: Ensuring legal compliance with leave and benefit programs.
- Key Laws: Family and Medical Leave Act (FMLA), Consolidated Omnibus Budget Reconciliation Act (COBRA).
- Other Considerations: Americans with Disabilities Act (ADA).

Miscellaneous

- Focus: Staying up-to-date on emerging legal issues.
- Examples: Drug testing and medical marijuana laws.

SHRM Proficiency Indicators

For All HR Professionals:

- Stay updated on U.S. employment laws.
- Ensure HR practices comply with relevant laws.
- Educate employees on legal rights and prevent discrimination.
- Seek legal counsel when needed.

For Advanced HR Professionals:

- Maintain in-depth knowledge of employment law.
- Establish compliance programs and monitor adherence.
- Advise leadership on legal and regulatory risks.
- Oversee legal compliance of HR programs and technologies.

We'd Love Your Feedback!

Please let us know how we're doing by leaving us a review.

Quiz Corner 12 - WORKPLACE KNOWLEDGE DOMAIN

Stand-alone Knowledge-Based Questions:

1. What are examples of HR structures that support global work?

A) Diversity initiatives and cultural sensitivity training
B) International business travel policies and geographic centers of excellence
C) Local recruitment strategies and employee assistance programs
D) Workplace safety regulations and labor union agreements

2. Which act governs employment authorization and requires completion of Form I-9?

A) Fair Labor Standards Act (FLSA)
B) Occupational Safety and Health Act (OSHA)
C) Immigration Reform and Control Act of 1986
D) Americans with Disabilities Act (ADA)

3. What are examples of risk treatments in enterprise risk management?

A) Acceptance and exposure
B) Avoidance and ignorance
C) Sharing and retention
D) Elimination and confrontation

4. Which legislation mandates employers to provide lactation rooms for nursing mothers?

A) Family and Medical Leave Act (FMLA)
B) Affordable Care Act (ACA)
C) Americans with Disabilities Act (ADA)
D) Drug-Free Workplace Act

5. What is the primary purpose of Corporate Social Responsibility (CSR)?

A) Maximizing shareholder profits
B) Fulfilling legal obligations
C) Operating ethically and contributing to community development
D) Minimizing environmental impact

Quiz Corner 12 - WORKPLACE KNOWLEDGE DOMAIN

Scenario-Based Situational Judgment Questions:

1. **Situation:** A multinational corporation plans to expand its operations to a new country. What steps would you take as the HR manager to ensure successful international employee assignments?

A) Offer language training and rental subsidies to employees
B) Develop a comprehensive strategy addressing cultural integration and compensation adjustments
C) Implement strict immigration controls and minimize cross-border collaboration
D) Avoid international assignments due to potential legal complications

2. **Situation:** Your organization is experiencing an increase in workplace accidents. What measures would you implement as an HR professional to address safety concerns?

A) Enforce stricter disciplinary actions for safety violations
B) Conduct thorough safety training and hazard identification programs
C) Ignore the issue until it resolves itself
D) Limit employee access to safety equipment

3. **Situation:** Your organization wants to improve its corporate social responsibility (CSR) initiatives. What approach would you suggest to effectively integrate CSR into the company's culture?

a) A) Implement CSR activities without informing employees
B) Develop a CSR strategy aligned with the organization's mission and values
C) Ignore CSR initiatives as they have little impact on organizational success
D) Outsource CSR activities to third-party organizations

4. **Situation:** Your organization faces legal challenges related to employment law compliance. As an advanced HR professional, what steps would you take to ensure organizational compliance?

A) Ignore legal challenges and focus on other HR functions
B) Establish criteria for compliance with relevant laws and regulations
C) Seek legal counsel only when legal challenges escalate
D) Delegate compliance responsibilities to lower-level HR staff

5. **Situation:** Your organization is considering expanding its workforce globally. What factors would you consider to ensure successful global workforce management?

A) Limit cross-border collaboration to minimize risks
B) Develop a comprehensive organizational strategy addressing global workforce issues
C) Avoid international assignments due to potential complications
D) Implement standardized HR programs without considering local needs

Quiz Corner 12 - WORKPLACE KNOWLEDGE DOMAIN

Stand-alone Knowledge-Based Questions:

1. B) International business travel policies and geographic centers of excellence
2. C) Immigration Reform and Control Act of 1986
3. C) Sharing and retention
4. B) Affordable Care Act (ACA)
5. C) Operating ethically and contributing to community development

Scenario-Based Situational Judgment Questions:

1. B) Develop a comprehensive strategy addressing cultural integration and compensation adjustments(Option B is correct because it aligns with best practices for international assignments, including cultural integration, compensation adjustments, and comprehensive strategies.)
2. B) Conduct thorough safety training and hazard identification programs(Option B is the correct choice as it aligns with best practices for addressing workplace safety concerns by implementing safety training and hazard identification programs.)
3. B) Develop a CSR strategy aligned with the organization's mission and values(Explanation for Type B Question 8: Option B is the correct choice as it aligns with best practices for integrating CSR into the company's culture effectively by developing a strategy aligned with the organization's mission and values.)
4. B) Establish criteria for compliance with relevant laws and regulations(Option B is the correct choice as it aligns with best practices for ensuring organizational compliance by establishing criteria for compliance with relevant laws and regulations.)
5. B) Develop a comprehensive organizational strategy addressing global workforce issues(Option B is the correct choice as it aligns with best practices for successful global workforce management by developing a comprehensive organizational strategy addressing global workforce issues.)

9. Appendix

GLOSSARY

Behavioral Competencies:

Leadership and Navigation:

- Navigating the Organization: Ability to understand and navigate the organizational structure, dynamics, and culture effectively.
- Vision: Capacity to articulate and communicate a compelling vision for the organization's future.
- Managing HR Initiatives: Skill in leading and managing human resources initiatives to achieve organizational goals.
- Influence: Ability to influence and persuade others to achieve desired outcomes ethically.

Ethical Practice:

- Personal Integrity: Commitment to maintaining personal integrity and ethical conduct in all professional interactions.
- Professional Integrity: Dedication to upholding professional standards of integrity and ethical behavior.
- Ethical Agent: Capacity to act as an ethical agent by identifying and addressing ethical issues within the organization.

Diversity, Equity & Inclusion (DE&I):

- Creating a Diverse and Inclusive Culture: Ability to foster a workplace culture that values and embraces diversity and inclusion.
- Ensuring Equity Effectiveness: Promoting equity and fairness in organizational policies, practices, and decision-making.
- Connecting DE&I to Organizational Performance: Understanding of how diversity, equity, and inclusion initiatives contribute to organizational success.

Relationship Management:

- Networking: Ability to build and maintain professional relationships and networks.
- Relationship Building: Skill in cultivating and nurturing positive relationships with colleagues, stakeholders, and partners.
- Teamwork: Capacity to collaborate effectively with others to achieve common goals.

Communication:

- Delivering Messages: Ability to communicate effectively to diverse audiences using appropriate channels and mediums.
- Exchanging Organizational Information: Skill in facilitating the exchange of information within the organization to enhance collaboration and decision-making.
- Listening: Capacity to actively listen and understand others' perspectives, needs, and concerns.

Global Mindset:

- Operating in a Culturally Diverse Workplace: Ability to work effectively in a culturally diverse environment, respecting and valuing differences.
- Operating in a Global Environment: Understanding global business dynamics, cultures, and trends.
- Advocating for a Culturally Diverse and Inclusive Workplace: We are committed to promoting diversity, equity, and inclusion in a global context.

Business Acumen:

- Business and Competitive Awareness: Understanding the organization's industry, market, competitors, and business environment.
- Business Analysis: Skill in analyzing business data, trends, and performance metrics to inform decision-making.
- Strategic Alignment: Ability to align HR strategies and initiatives with the organization's strategic objectives.

Consultation:

- Evaluating Business Challenges: Skill in assessing organizational challenges and opportunities from a strategic HR perspective.
- Designing HR Solutions: Ability to develop customized HR solutions to address specific organizational needs.
- Advising on HR Solutions: Capacity to provide expert advice and guidance on HR-related matters to organizational leaders.
- Change Management: Skill in managing organizational change effectively, including communication, stakeholder engagement, and implementation.

Analytical Aptitude:

- Data Advocate: Advocacy for using data-driven approaches in HR decision-making and strategy development.
- Data Gathering: Skill in collecting and analyzing relevant data to inform HR practices and initiatives.
- Data Analysis: Ability to interpret and analyze HR-related data to identify trends, patterns, and insights.
- Evidence-Based Decision-Making: Capacity to make informed decisions based on empirical evidence and data analysis.

People Knowledge Domain:

HR Strategy:

- Strategic HR Planning: Aligning HR strategies with organizational goals and objectives.
- Talent Management: Strategies and practices for attracting, developing, and retaining top talent.
- Succession Planning: Process of identifying and developing future leaders within the organization.
- Workforce Planning: Forecasting and planning for the organization's future workforce needs.

Talent Acquisition:

- Recruitment: Process of sourcing, attracting, and selecting candidates for vacant positions within the organization.
- Selection: Procedures and methods used to assess and choose the most qualified candidates for specific roles.
- Onboarding integrates new employees into the organization and provides them with the necessary resources and information to succeed.

Employee Engagement & Retention:

- Employee Engagement: Strategies and initiatives aimed at enhancing employees' commitment, motivation, and satisfaction.
- Retention Strategies: Practices and programs designed to reduce turnover and retain top talent within the organization.
- Recognition and Rewards: Programs to acknowledge and reward employees for their contributions and achievements.

Learning & Development:

- Training and Development: Activities and programs designed to enhance employees' skills, knowledge, and competencies.
- Career Development: Initiatives to support employees' career growth and advancement within the organization.
- Leadership Development: Programs aimed at developing leadership skills and capabilities at all levels of the organization.

Total Rewards:

- Compensation: Strategies and practices related to employee compensation and benefits design and administration.
- Benefits Administration: Management of employee benefits programs, including health insurance, retirement plans, and other perks.
- Recognition Programs: Initiatives to acknowledge and reward employees for their contributions and achievements beyond monetary compensation.

Organization Knowledge Domain:

Structure of the HR Function:
- HR Department Structure: Design and organization of the HR department within the organization.
- HR Service Delivery Models: Methods and approaches for delivering HR services to employees and stakeholders.
- HR Technology: Technology and HRIS systems streamline HR processes and enhance efficiency.

Organizational Effectiveness & Development:
- Organizational Development (OD): Strategies and interventions to improve organizational effectiveness and performance.
- Change Management: Techniques and processes for managing organizational change and transition effectively.
- Culture Change: Initiatives to shift and transform organizational culture to align with strategic goals and objectives.

Workforce Management:
- Workforce Planning: Forecasting and planning for the organization's future workforce needs.
- Staffing and Deployment: Allocation and deployment of employees to various organizational roles and positions.
- Workforce Analytics: Analysis of workforce data and metrics to inform decision-making and improve workforce management practices.

Employee & Labor Relations:
- Employee Relations: Managing relationships between employees and the organization, including conflict resolution and grievance handling.
- Labor Relations: Interaction and negotiation with labor unions and collective bargaining units within the organization.
- Compliance with Employment Laws: Ensuring compliance with relevant employment laws and regulations to maintain a positive work environment and mitigate legal risks.

Technology Management:

- HRIS Implementation: Planning, selecting, and implementing HRIS systems to support HR functions and processes.
- Technology Integration: Integration of HR technology solutions with other organizational systems and processes.
- Data Security and Privacy: Protection of HR data and information from unauthorized access and breaches.

Workplace Knowledge Domain:

Managing a Global Workforce:

- Global Mobility: Management of international assignments, expatriate programs, and cross-border workforce issues.
- Immigration and Visa Management: This includes compliance with immigration laws and regulations and managing visa processes for international employees.
- Cross-Cultural Communication: Communication and collaboration with employees and stakeholders from diverse cultural backgrounds.

Risk Management:

- Enterprise Risk Management (ERM): Identifying, assessing, and mitigating organizational risks.
- Workplace Safety: Implementing policies and procedures to ensure the safety and well-being of employees in the workplace.
- Crisis Management: Preparation and response to crises and emergencies, including natural disasters, security threats, and pandemics.

Corporate Social Responsibility:

- CSR Strategy: Developing and implementing corporate social responsibility initiatives aligned with organizational values and goals.
- Community Engagement: Involvement in community projects, volunteerism, and philanthropic activities to support social and environmental causes.
- Sustainability Initiatives: Programs and practices aimed at reducing environmental impact and promoting sustainable business practices.

U.S. Employment Law & Regulations:

- Employment Discrimination: Compliance with laws and regulations prohibiting discrimination based on protected characteristics such as race, gender, age, and disability.
- Wage and Hour Laws: Compliance with laws governing minimum wage, overtime pay, and other compensation-related regulations.
- Workplace Health and Safety: Adherence to Occupational Safety and Health Administration (OSHA) regulations to ensure a safe and healthy work environment.

SAMPLE STUDY PLAN

Week	Domain	Topics	Activities
1	Workplace Knowledge (SHRM-CP)	Managing a Global Workforce	- Review SHRM Learning Objectives for these domains.
1	Workplace Knowledge (SHRM-CP)	Risk Management	- Read relevant chapters in SHRM study guide or textbook.
1	Strategic HR Management (SHRM-SCP)	Leadership Development	- Watch online lectures or webinars on these topics.
1	Strategic HR Management (SHRM-SCP)	Change Management	
2	Workplace Knowledge (SHRM-CP)	Corporate Social Responsibility (CSR)	- Focus on legal aspects of HR: FMLA, ADA, FLSA, etc.
2	Workplace Knowledge (SHRM-CP)	U.S. Employment Law & Regulations	- Research current trends in CSR and their impact on HR practices.
2	Business Acumen (SHRM-SCP)	Financial Statements	- Complete practice quizzes on legal topics.
2	Business Acumen (SHRM-SCP)	Marketing Strategies	
3	SHRM Knowledge, Skills & Abilities (SHRM-CP)	HR Strategy	- Explore talent management strategies (recruitment, retention, development).
3	SHRM Knowledge, Skills & Abilities (SHRM-CP)	Workforce Relations	- Learn effective conflict resolution techniques in the workplace.
3	Strategic HR Management (SHRM-SCP)	Employee Engagement	- Participate in online discussion forums on HR best practices.
3	Strategic HR Management (SHRM-SCP)	Organizational Culture	
4	SHRM Knowledge, Skills & Abilities (SHRM-CP)	Compensation and Benefits	- Learn different compensation structures and legal considerations.
4	SHRM Knowledge, Skills & Abilities (SHRM-CP)	Recruitment and Selection	- Explore various recruitment methods and selection processes.
4	Business Acumen (SHRM-SCP)	Risk Management Principles	- Practice writing job descriptions and interview questions.
4	Business Acumen (SHRM-SCP)	Mergers & Acquisitions	
5	Review & Practice (Both Exams)	Revisit all domains covered so far.	- Take full-length practice exams to identify strengths and weaknesses.
5	Review & Practice (Both Exams)		- Focus on areas requiring improvement based on practice test results.
6	SHRM Code of Ethics (Both Exams)	Review the SHRM Code of Ethics	- Analyze case studies involving ethical dilemmas in HR.
6	SHRM Code of Ethics (Both Exams)	Review the SHRM Code of Ethics	- Discuss ethical decision-making frameworks with fellow test-preppers.
7	Mock Exams & Review (Both Exams)	Participate in simulated exam environments	- Review answer explanations for practice exams, especially incorrect answers.
7	Mock Exams & Review (Both Exams)	with timed practice tests.	- Consult with instructors or mentors to address any lingering questions.
8	Final Review & Self-Care (Both Exams)	Focus on quick revisions of key concepts	- Prioritize sleep, healthy eating, and stress management for optimal performance.
8	Final Review & Self-Care (Both Exams)	Focus on quick revisions of key concepts	- Review testing center policies and logistics to avoid last-minute surprises.

CONCLUSION

Congratulations! You've reached the culmination of your dedicated efforts in preparing for the SHRM CP/SCP exam. This comprehensive guide has equipped you with the knowledge, strategies, and resources to confidently navigate the exam and demonstrate your mastery of HR practices.

Remember, passing the exam is just the beginning. The HR field is constantly evolving, so continuous learning is paramount. Here are some key takeaways to propel you forward in your HR career:

- **Stay Updated**: Remain current with the latest HR trends, legal developments, and best practices. Utilize resources from SHRM, industry publications, and professional development opportunities.

- **Embrace Continuous Learning**: Never stop expanding your HR knowledge. Pursue professional certifications, attend conferences and workshops, and engage in online learning platforms.

- **Develop Your Network**: Build strong relationships with fellow HR professionals, mentors, and industry leaders. A strong network can provide invaluable support and career guidance.

- **Sharpen Your Skills**: Possess your HR skills through practical experience, role-playing exercises, and case studies. Focus on developing critical thinking, problem-solving, and communication skills.

- **Embrace Ethical Leadership**: Uphold the highest ethical standards in your HR practices. Refer to the SHRM Code of Ethics and make well-informed decisions that prioritize the well-being of employees and the organization.

As you embark on your HR journey, remember that your commitment to professional growth and ethical leadership will pave the way for a successful and rewarding career.

We wish you the very best in achieving your HR goals and positively impacting the organizations you serve.

10. Sample Questions for the Exam

SAMPLE QUESTION SHRM CP

1. Which selection tool should be used to fill a vacancy that requires managing multiple priorities and working under pressure?

A. Cognitive ability test
B. Background check
C. Behavioral assessment
D. Academic transcript

2. Which action best fosters high ethical standards in an organization?

A. Establishing an anonymous reporting hotline
B. Adopting a corporate social responsibility policy
C. Providing manager training on codes of conduct
D. Distributing the employee handbook annually

3. When developing an emergency disaster plan, which activity occurs during a vulnerability analysis?

A. Determining the likelihood of potential hazards and their effects on the business
B. Identifying key products, services, and operations and evaluating their reinforcements
C. Assessing available internal and external resources and establishing emergency contacts
D. Working with an insurance carrier to analyze exclusions and areas of exposure

4. A VP of talent development requests a two-day communication skills training for the team. The VP and the trainer meet for a planning session. The VP explained that the department is working on several key projects and needs to improve its effective communication. During the training session, the trainer observed an apparent lack of trust and openness among team members, which caused some team members to withdraw from the training activities. The VP receives feedback from managers that indicates the session did not go well, so the VP requests a meeting with the trainer. After the training session is complete, which step should the trainer take?

A. Review the training evaluations for the session.
B. Debrief the VP on observations during training.
C. Meet with the team's supervisor to disclose findings.
D. Calculate the return on investment for the session.

5. A VP of talent development requests a two-day communication skills training for the team. The VP and the trainer meet for a planning session. The VP explains that the department is working on several key projects and needs to improve its effective communication to succeed. During the training session, the trainer observed an apparent lack of trust and openness among team members, which caused some team members to withdraw from the training activities. The VP receives feedback from managers that indicates the session did not go well, so the VP requests a meeting with the trainer. Which action should the trainer take to improve group dynamics?

A. Conduct a team performance appraisal.
B. Provide coaching to high-performing team members.
C. Assess levels of trust among team members.
D. Schedule an offsite team-building activity.

SAMPLE QUESTION SHRM CP

6. .Several raters evaluate job descriptions and arrange them according to their value to the company. Which job evaluation method are the raters using?

A. Classification
B. Ranking
C. Point factor
D. Market-pricing

7. Which strategy best facilitates internal transfers and maximizes flexibility when assigning pay levels?

A. Adjusting pay based on comparable worth of jobs
B. Minimizing overlap between pay grades
C. Implementing a broadband pay system
D. Adopting a seniority-based pay system

8. Which activity best exemplifies job enrichment?

A. An IT employee researches how to resolve a software problem.
B. A marketing employee spends extra time developing new branding ideas.
C. A billing department employee is given the added responsibility of calculating payroll.
D. A sales employee is selected by a supervisor to mentor junior employees.

9 . Three product leads from a software company's research and development division meet with an HR manager to discuss the performance problems of a project manager. Each product lead reports encountering similar issues with the project manager. The biggest problem is that the project manager consistently promises products will be completed by a specific date and fails to deliver. During the discussion, the three product leads complained about losing customers due to the project manager's behaviors. Six months after the initial consultation with the HR manager, the division director asks for an update on the project manager's progress. How should the HR manager present this data?

A. Prepare a detailed performance summary for each project over the past six months.
B. Schedule a meeting so the product leads can share data about customer retention with the division director.
C. Focus on the project manager's progress toward time and budget metrics over the last six months.
D. Submit a report with detailed notes from the project manager's performance meetings.

10 . Three product leads from a software company's research and development division meet with an HR manager to discuss the performance problems of a project manager. Each product lead reports encountering similar issues with the project manager. The biggest problem is that the project manager consistently promises products will be completed by a specific date and fails to deliver. During the discussion, the three product leads complained about losing customers due to the project manager's behaviors. The project manager says managing multiple large projects is too difficult. Which strategy should the HR manager use to address this issue best?

A. Hire a project coordinator to handle administrative project tasks.
B. Assign the project manager with a mentor to provide advice and assistance.
C. Help the project manager break large tasks into smaller, more manageable pieces.
D. Ask the project manager's supervisor to delegate projects to other employees temporarily.

ANSWER: SAMPLE QUESTION SHRM CP

1. The correct answer is "C: Behavioral assessment."

Behavioral assessments evaluate a candidate's personality profile and work style. Cognitive ability tests measure intelligence, verbal ability, math skills, spatial perception, and reasoning. Background checks verify prior employment, education, and criminal background information. Academic transcripts only outline academic performance.

2. The correct answer is "C: Providing manager training on codes of conduct."

Training managers on codes of conduct helps managers understand and promote ethical behavior, fostering high ethical standards. Establishing an anonymous reporting hotline does not help employees understand the company's ethical standards, so they cannot effectively use it. Corporate social responsibility policies generally focus on a company's external commitment to operate ethically and contribute to economic development. Distributing the employee handbook annually does not guarantee that employees read or understand its contents.

3. The correct answer is "A: Determining the likelihood of potential hazards and their effects on the business."

To conduct a vulnerability analysis, a company must examine the hazards within the company and the community in which the business is located and consider crises that have occurred in the past or may result from the geographic location of the business or technological or human error. The business should then determine the likelihood of facing those hazards and the severity of the consequences they would have on the business. The other response options are appropriate risk management activities to execute but do not specifically support a vulnerability analysis.

4. The correct answer is "A: Review the training evaluations."

Situational judgment tests evaluate an examinee's ability to identify the best course of action from available options. Best practices should be followed, not specific organizational approaches. SHRM-certified experts evaluate each option for effectiveness to determine the best response.

5. The correct answer is "C: Assess levels of trust among team members."

Panels of SHRM-certified subject matter experts rate the effectiveness of each SJI response option, and the "best" answer is derived by statistical analysis of those expert opinions.

ANSWER: SAMPLE QUESTION SHRM CP

6. The correct answer is "B: Ranking"

Job evaluation methods include ranking, point factor, classification, and market pricing. The ranking is qualitative, while the point factor is quantitative. Classification is a qualitative technique, and market pricing emphasizes external competitiveness using compensation survey data.

7. The correct answer is "C: Implementing a broadband pay system."

Job evaluation methods include ranking, point factor, classification, and market pricing. Ranking is qualitative, while point factor is quantitative. Classification is a qualitative technique, and market pricing emphasizes external competitiveness using compensation survey data.

8. The correct answer is "D: A sales employee is selected by a supervisor to mentor junior employees."

Job enrichment occurs when a sales employee mentors others to learn new skills for a deeper job purpose. Job enhancement involves adding new skills to an existing base of knowledge. Job crafting involves redesigning daily tasks and duties, while job enlargement involves taking on extra responsibilities that are lateral to the current job.

9. The correct answer is "A: Prepare a detailed performance summary for each project over the past six months."

Panels of SHRM-certified subject matter experts rate the effectiveness of each SJI response option, and the "best" answer is derived by statistical analysis of those expert opinions.

10. The correct answer is "C: Help the project manager break large tasks into smaller, more manageable pieces."

Panels of SHRM-certified subject matter experts rate the effectiveness of each SJI response option, and the "best" answer is derived by statistical analysis of those expert opinions.

SAMPLE QUESTION SHRM SCP

1. An HR manager prepares for a budget meeting with multiple teams to determine departmental budget allocations. Which bargaining strategy should the HR manager use to achieve a mutually beneficial decision?

A. Distributive
B. Integrative
C. Zero-sum
D. Positional

2. A CEO requests people analytics data After recently implementing a new human capital management platform. Which action should the HR manager take first?

A. Direct the HR analyst to extract and summarize relevant data.
B. Develop a suite of analytical reports that focus on employee performance.
C. Train interested stakeholders on self-service options and decentralized capabilities.
D. Ask business partners to identify key metrics that link business strategy to outcomes.

3. Besides projected cost savings, which should be a primary consideration when determining whether to outsource a business function?

A. Rate of customer acquisition
B. Effect on employee morale
C. Timeline and action plan
D. Organization size

4. An HR manager meets with the area supervisor and an employee who has limited head mobility due to a work-related injury to discuss potential accommodations. The employee suggests building steps at one of the workstations in an assembly line so the employee does not have to look upward. After considering other workers' traffic patterns, everyone except the employee concludes that adding stairs will introduce a tripping hazard and decrease the safety of other workers. The employee threatened to file a lawsuit, claiming the company did not adequately explore the employee's suggested accommodation. Which action should the HR manager take to reduce the likelihood that the employee will file a lawsuit?

A. Place stairs on the assembly line temporarily so the workers can see the danger they pose to other workers.
B. Obtain a professional safety engineering analysis of the impact and feasibility of building the steps.
C. Ask other workers whether the steps will be hazardous before concluding the review.
D. Allow the employee to use the stairs under the condition that they will be removed if other employees complain about them.

5. An HR manager meets with the area supervisor and an employee who has limited head mobility due to a work-related injury to discuss potential accommodations. The employee suggests building steps at one of the workstations in an assembly line so the employee does not have to look upward. After considering other workers' traffic patterns, everyone except the employee concludes that adding stairs will introduce a tripping hazard and decrease the safety of other workers. The employee threatened to file a lawsuit, claiming the company did not adequately explore the employee's suggested accommodation. Senior management instructs the HR manager to develop a plan for legally terminating other injured employees to prevent them from filing suits. How should the HR manager respond?

A. Inform senior management that this action could result in the filing of wrongful termination suits.
B. Explain that other employees will observe the common theme among the terminated employees, which will lower the morale and trust of leadership.
C. Advise senior management to have the issue reviewed by a different team to see whether they can suggest alternate solutions.
D. Examine the employees' HR files to see whether there are any violations of company policy.

SAMPLE QUESTION SHRM SCP

6. A CEO asks the VP of HR to recommend talent-rich countries for global expansion and consider cost as part of the recommendation. When identifying potential countries, which is most important for the VP of HR to consider?

A. Each country's employment laws and regulations
B. Availability and compatibility of HRIS platforms
C. The company's readiness to deploy expatriates
D. Cultural and language training needs

7. A talent director at a global apparel company is designing an employee value proposition (EVP) to grow the external candidate pipeline. Which action should the talent director take first?

A. Develop separate and distinct branding for the EVP that is different from the marketing brand to avoid confusing candidates.
B. Create unique EVP brand and recruitment campaign materials for each region across the global organization to appeal to local audiences.
C. Engage with external vendors to minimize bias and ensure cultural sensitivity in EVP recruitment campaign materials.
D. Partner with the marketing team to build an EVP and associated recruiting campaigns that align with the company's core brand.

8. When developing leave plans, which factors are the most critical to consider?

A. Objectives and legal requirements
B. Types and employment eligibility
C. Cost and budgetary implications
D. Policies and procedures for use

9. An organization's outdated HRIS is difficult to use and involves a paper-and-pen performance rating process. The organization is headquartered in a storm-prone area. During a recent weather-related evacuation, employees could not complete and submit performance ratings in a timely manner. The HR department selects a new online HRIS vendor to mitigate this issue in the future.

Leadership agrees to fund the new HRIS, which includes employee self-service features. Which action should the HR director take to encourage employees to use the HRIS?

A. Reinforce the benefits of using the self-service features, including immediate access to information.
B. Show employees the self-service features when they ask HR to provide basic information.
C. Explain that the employee self-service features will save time for the HR department.
D. Provide in-person and virtual training on the new HRIS employee self-service features.

10. An organization's outdated HRIS is difficult to use and involves a paper-and-pen performance rating process. The organization is headquartered in a storm-prone area. During a recent weather-related evacuation, employees could not complete and submit performance ratings in a timely manner. The HR department selects a new online HRIS vendor to mitigate this issue in the future.

At performance review time, employees express anxiety over the security of their online ratings. Which action should the HR director take in response to these concerns?

A. Share statistics about the likelihood and effects of a cybersecurity breach in the new HRIS.
B. Allow concerned employees to complete their ratings on paper rather than online.
C. Create a contingency plan that outlines corrective actions the company will take if a breach occurs.
D. Ask a representative from the HRIS company to describe the company's data security processes and protections.

ANSWER: SAMPLE QUESTION SHRM SCP

1. The correct answer is "B: Integrative."

Integrative negotiation seeks mutually beneficial solutions. It's different from distributive and zero-sum bargaining, which are "win-lose." Positional bargaining is adversarial, leading to negative feelings.

2. The correct answer is "D: Ask business partners to identify key metrics that link business strategy to outcomes."

By asking the business partners to identify key metrics that link business strategy to outcomes, the HR manager understands the most important information needed from the analytics data. The HR manager can then decide on the best way to extract, analyze, and communicate that data. After identifying the key metrics that should be measured, summarizing data, developing analytical reports, and training stakeholders are important actions to take.

3. The correct answer is "B: Effect on employee morale."

Outsourcing can affect employee morale, leading to increased voluntary turnover and reduced innovation. When selecting a vendor, consider the customer acquisition rate to ensure they can meet your needs. Develop a timeline and action plan to ensure a smooth transition. Outsourcing is appropriate for organizations of all sizes and should be considered based on individual circumstances.

4. The correct answer is "B: Obtain a professional safety engineering analysis of the impact and feasibility of building the steps."

Situational judgment requires the examinee to think about what is occurring in the scenario and decide which response option identifies the most effective course of action. Other response options may be something you could do to respond to the situation, but SJIs require thinking and action based on the best of the available options. Do not base your answer on your organization's approach to handling the situation, but rather, answer based on what you know should be done according to best practice. Panels of SHRM-certified subject matter experts rate the effectiveness of each response option, and the "best" answer is derived by statistical analysis of those expert opinions.

5. The correct answer is "A: Inform senior management that this action could result in the filing of wrongful termination suits."

Panels of SHRM-certified subject matter experts rate the effectiveness of each SJI response option, and the "best" answer is derived by statistical analysis of those expert opinions.

6. The correct answer is "A: Each country's employment laws and regulations."

The VP of HR should assess each country's legal requirements to determine the total cost of salaries, benefits, work obligations, etc. Adopting an HRIS platform can mitigate the availability and compatibility issues. Migrating to HRIS has a lower one-time cost than recurring employee expenses. Expatriates and language training are not required for transborder expansion into a talent-rich country.

7. The correct answer is "D: Partner with the marketing team to build an EVP and associated recruiting campaigns that align with the company's core brand."

The talent director should partner with the marketing team to build an EVP and associated recruiting campaigns that align with the company's core brand to sustain the brand and ensure consistency over time. Developing separate and distinct branding for either the EVP or each region will dilute the brand and create an inconsistent message. Engaging with external vendors to ensure the EVP materials are culturally sensitive is an important step, but it is not the first step.

ANSWER: SAMPLE QUESTION SHRM SCP

8. The correct answer is "A: Objectives and legal requirements."

When developing leave plans, HR should first consider why the organization is considering a paid leave program (i.e., the objectives) and applicable legal requirements that mandate the employer to provide paid leave.

Identifying leave types, employment eligibility, policies and procedures for use, cost, and budgetary considerations should be considered after the leave objectives and legal requirements are identified.

9. The correct answer is "A: Reinforce the benefits of using the self-service features, including immediate access to information."

Panels of SHRM-certified subject matter experts rate the effectiveness of each SJI response option, and the "best" answer is derived by statistical analysis of those expert opinions.

10. The correct answer is "D: Ask a representative from the HRIS company to describe the company's data security processes and protections."

Panels of SHRM-certified subject matter experts rate the effectiveness of each SJI response option, and the "best" answer is derived by statistical analysis of those expert opinions.

www.ingramcontent.com/pod-product-compliance
Lightning Source LLC
Chambersburg PA
CBHW082207070526
44585CB00020B/2324